Allan Eric, partner Junior

Following the Tow-Path and Through the Adirondacks

Awheel

Allan Eric, partner Junior

Following the Tow-Path and Through the Adirondacks Awheel

ISBN/EAN: 9783744746892

Printed in Europe, USA, Canada, Australia, Japan

Cover: Foto ©Andreas Hilbeck / pixelio.de

More available books at **www.hansebooks.com**

The Junior Partner

FOLLOWING THE TOW-PATH

AND

Through the Adirondacks Awheel.

BY

ALLAN ERIC

AND

THE "JUNIOR PARTNER."

Authors of:—"Buckra" Land, The Old Well of Cartagena,
A Vacation Tour Awheel, Etc.

1898.

BOSTON:
N. E. R. G. Publishing Co.

1898,
BY THE AUTHORS.

LIST OF ILLUSTRATIONS.

The "Junior Partner"	Frontispiece.
	Page.
Western Portal of the Hoosac Tunnel	11
On the Cinder Path	16
A Curious Road	18
Lock on the Erie Canal	24
A Lock-Keeper and Family	26
View on the Erie Canal	28
Scene in the Mohawk Valley	34
View on the Mohawk River	42
On the Aqueduct, Erie Canal	47
On the Tow-Path, Erie Canal	50
Congress Park, Saratoga	52
An Adirondack Lake	55
Stuck in the Sand	67
View on Lake Champlain	80
The "Ethan Allen"	82
A Vermont Road	90

FOLLOWING THE TOW-PATH

AND THROUGH

THE ADIRONDACKS AWHEEL.

CHAPTER I.

AFTER months of consultation and deliberation with regard to various routes for our second bicycle tour, we decided that the one best suited to the time at our disposal would be out through the Mohawk Valley, in New York State, famed for its beauty, thence northward to the lake and Adirondack region; and east, to Lake Champlain, that great inland sea of historic fame, which spreads across the boundary between the states of New York and Vermont, and stretches north to the Canadian border.

With the aid of maps and our own knowledge of those regions, we had little difficulty in approximately laying out the route; but, concerning the roads that we might expect to encounter, we were unable to obtain any information. However, as tourists, we did not hesitate to set out, and we did so with a grim determination to adhere to the route, let come what might, and take things as they came, resolving to find pleasure in every incident which might be in store for us.

The route planned was certainly a unique one, somewhat outside of the beaten track, which was one great attraction for us; and we knew that we should see many interesting things, new life, and some of the most beautiful scenery on the continent.

On our former tour we wheeled west from Boston to within about 35 miles of Albany, so this time we thought it advisable not to use up our time wheeling over the same route. We therefore, the Junior Partner and I, decided to go by rail to Albany and take our departure awheel from the capital city of the Empire State.

So, one beautiful, bright July morning found us luxuriously installed in a cool, comfortable car of the Fitchburg Railroad, and at 9.30 o'clock the splendid train pulled out of the Union Station. Our wheels, touring-case and the canvas case containing a reserve supply of clothing, which was to go ahead of us throughout the trip, were in the baggage car; and in the car with us were the camera, a small bundle which later would be carried on one of the wheels, and my pith helmet, which I had worn in the West Indies, and which I proposed wearing on this trip to protect my head from the direct heat of the sun.

The experience of the combined luxury of the travel on the Fitchburg Railroad, through the unsurpassed scenery of Massachusetts, ever-changing, now of gentle, quiet beauty, and, as we approach the northwestern part of the State, gradually merging into mountain grandeur, was not new to us.

And yet it is ever new, for how can we tire of the beautiful in nature! The train flew swiftly along, first past the lovely towns joining and nearby Boston; past magnificent estates and blossoming gardens; across streams, skirting placid little lakes and flowering meadows; through rich intervales and past fertile farms that enjoy a high state of cultivation. It was the beginning of the haying season, and the luxuriant grass was being laid low by the mowing machine, and busy workers were everywhere seen. Now we would pass a field of strawberries, where men, women and children were engaged in gathering the luscious fruit from the vines; and then, on either side, the hills and dales were covered, some with yellow daisies, and others with white ones, the latter looking not unlike a mantle of snow. Flowers grew in profusion along the line of the railroad, of many kinds and colors.

The first stop of the train was at Ayer, but in a few minutes it was speeding on again toward the Connecticut river valley, and we scarcely realized that we were making such rapid progress ere we were crossing the broad Connecticut river, when we were afforded a fine view down that famed valley, whose rich alluvial lands are among the most productive in the whole country.

"Greenfield!" called the train-men. That word is ever a welcome sound, for here the train stops for lunch, and the passengers lose no time in placing themselves in close touch with the excellent eatables there to be secured. Those who do not care to leave the train are waited upon by courteous young men, and are able to enjoy an acceptable lunch quietly in the car.

As the train pulled out of Greenfield I sought the luxurious smoking apartment of the parlor car, while the Junior Partner occupied herself with a book and a box of ice-cream. The country had now changed its aspect, and the foot-hills, then the Hoosac Mountains themselves rose on either side. Covered with thick foliage for the most part—though an occasional rugged crag frowned down upon the fair valleys—there was a delicious freshness after the showers of the evening before, which rendered the pictures flitting by even more pleasing. Now and then the train would roar over a bridge which spanned the Deerfield river, which now gently flowing and then foaming over a stony bed, appeared first on one side and then on the other. Again we were gazing down upon the Deerfield Valley, fair as the Garden of Eden, and then we were shut in by the mountains that now towered yet higher. Once in a while we caught a glimpse of a bit of the highway which wound along between the mountains, and here and there a quiet farm-house nestling in a mountain nook.

When the train passed Zoar I left the smoking apartment, for the famous Hoosac Tunnel would soon be reached, and we never tire of the experience, and always make the most of it. The train hands came through the cars and closed all the ventilators and lighted the lamps. Looking from the windows we could now and then, as the train swung around a sharp curve, as it threaded its way in and out among the mountains, see the great locomotive as it pursued its ponderous way, sending up columns of black smoke from its stack.

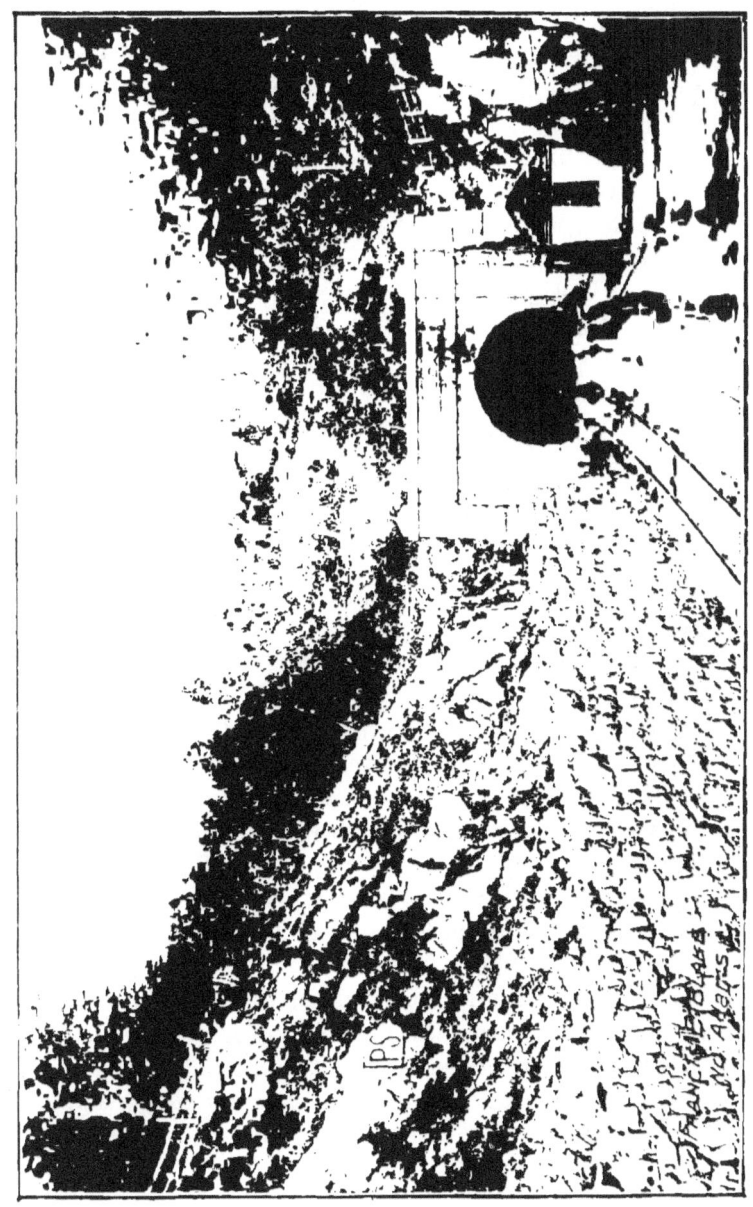

Hoosac Tunnel station was left behind, and then we watched for the great archway of the eastern portal of the tunnel. A few more curves, and then the locomotive, as though weary of turning aside for the mountains, seemed to charge the last mighty base, and then we went in out of the sunlight, and the train roared and the echoes roared back as we rushed securely along beneath the mountain, through its very vitals, pierced by the energy of man, with thousands of feet of rock above us. The great bore is nearly five miles long, and beside being one of the most celebrated railroad tunnels in the world, it is probably the safest, for it is bored through solid rock, which forms the everlasting foundation of the Hoosac Mountains.

Once more in the bright sunlight the Hoosacs are left behind, and before us were the Berkshire Hills, less grand but more beautiful than the mightier range.

A brief stop at North Adams, then another at Williamstown, and we sped across a corner of the State of Vermont before crossing the line into New York. Shortly before reaching Troy, where we made a brief stop to see if our laundry was ready, the section of the train which was bound for Saratoga dropped us; for the Fitchburg Road is the main highway from New England to Saratoga and the adjacent lovely region of lakes and mountains.

Soon we caught a first sight of the Erie Canal, near its eastern terminus, and we eagerly looked at the tow-path to see what it was like, for we intended to wheel over some sections of it later on. The canal seemed to be full of water to the very edges, and here and there the squatty-looking boats were drawn up discharging cargo.

Reaching Albany we went at once to our hotel, where we removed the dust of travel, and then started out to see a little of the city. Noticing steps leading up to the end of the railroad bridge near by, which here spans the Hudson river between Albany and Rensselaer, we ascended them, and walked out on the footway along beside the tracks, to about the centre of the bridge, when we had a fine view of the broad Hudson, up and down, with its traffic of steamers and other craft; including one of the palatial steamers that ply between Albany and New York City. We next visited the Capitol, of which we had heard so much. State street leads up to it. It consists of a huge pile of brick and stone, but the style of architecture is more fitting for a magnificent hotel than for the Capitol of a great state. We were not impressed by it, as a whole; but the grounds surrounding it are fine, and the grand esplanade and the main entrance to the building are superb, some fine sculptures being grouped around the latter, but which cannot be fully appreciated except by a careful examination in detail.

We entered the Capitol, and were surprised to find, on the street floor of the immense pile, all sorts of establishments foreign to state departments. "Guides" lurk in the dimly-lighted corridors, and to even glance at one of them is to have him pounce upon you and urge the importance of his services. Even if you do not look at them you will be lucky if you escape. After taking a glance around at the dim corridors, we concluded that the only guide we should want would be a compass. However, we quickly found what we were in search of—the office of the Superintendent of Public Works, for we wished to inquire particularly as to whether there was any objection to our riding on the tow-path of the canal, and to obtain other information. We were very pleasantly received by the Superintendent, who paid us particular attention, explaining that we were at liberty to ride on the tow-path, provided we would take things as they came, which meant that we might now and then encounter men with rough edges, connected with the canal boats. The official, before we went out, kindly presented us with a set of maps, in a substantial cover, of the entire canal system, giving its course, locks, levels and stations, a very valuable possession.

After supper we rode completely around the city on an "A" Belt Line electric car, obtaining a good idea of how the capital looks. It is, on the whole, a very pretty, enterprising, and lively city; but the streets are a terror to cyclists, for they are nearly all paved with cobble stones, though we saw several paved with bricks. This was quite a novelty to us, but it makes a very acceptable street for the wheelman.

We left the car at Washington Park, which is a lovely piece of greenery, with fine trees and a pretty lake and fountain. In the twilight we sat and watched the people promenading, driving, and cycling, until the cyclists lighted their lamps and the "silent steeds" were gliding along, each with its one bright eye of fire flashing upon the shrubbery and across the road as the noiseless tires of inflated rubber sped over the smooth gravel roads.

We walked back down town, and after making a few inquiries as to the road by which we should leave the city in the morning, finally deciding to follow the cinder cycle path, fifteen miles in length, to Schenectady, constructed by the wheelmen, we returned to the hotel to secure a good night's rest, for to-morrow we would mount the wheels and begin the long and interesting tour awheel which we had laid out.

CHAPTER II.

Albany to Schenectady, Over the Bicycle Cinder-Path.—First Sight of the Erie Canal.—Following the Tow-Path.—Canal Boats and Tow-Horses.—Domestic Life on the Canal.

WE arose at an early hour—for us—the next morning, and, having had breakfast, after I had deposited enough cash with the hotel clerk to pay the water-tax for the next six months, we gathered up our effects and set out for the railroad station by an unnecessarily circuitous route, as it proved, where we secured our wheels from the baggage room and at once set to work fastening the luggage to the two bicycles. The touring case, which is seen in the engravings, going upon my Victor, also the foot-pump, which was strapped to the frame, and the camera on the handle bar. A bundle of necessary miscellaneous articles was fastened under the saddle of the Junior Partner's Victoria. The baggage master at the station was very courteous and obliging, and quite an audience gathered around to watch the expedition get under way. Everything secure, all the bearings were carefully oiled, and we started. We found it necessary to purchase a new carrier for the camera, and spent nearly two hours visiting the different bicycle stores in search of such a one as we required, but without success. We found some of different styles, most of them being apparently designed for taking babies out for a spin. Whether or not this was an indication of the popular requirement and demand in the line of luggage carriers in Albany we could not say, but it was not until we applied at a hardware store that we found what we required.

Now we were off, following Central avenue in a northwesterly direction out of the city. For some distance Central avenue is paved with brick, an easy surface over which to ride a wheel. At the outskirts of the city we turned sharply to the left and entered the fifteen-mile-long cycle path, which extends from Albany to Schenectady. It was constructed by the wheelmen, and its surface is covered by coal cinders, which pack very hard, making a track over which the wheels spin, giving a delightful sensation to the rider. The morning was bright and the sky was clear. The path, beside the apology for a main highway between the two cities, followed close to the walls and fences, and beneath overhanging trees, which afforded delightful shade for most of the way. Now and then the cycle path passed through tall grass, and now through low bushes and shrubbery, which would brush us as we glided on. All along the way the roadside was sprinkled with white and yellow daisies, and the fields and pastures were dotted with many wild flowers.

The highway, so-called, attracted our undivided attention, and several times we dismounted in order that we might more fully feast our eyes upon this "natural wonder," and thank our stars that there was such a thing as a cinder path; for, in the entire distance from Albany to Schenectady, there is not

a single rod of this road which could be ridden on a wheel. It is sand, deep sand for the whole fifteen miles, except at rare intervals, when the sand is varied by a short strip of rough road, over which light artillery would pass with extreme difficulty.

The only objectionable feature about the cycle path is that it is not wide enough for two to ride abreast; but we mention this only in a descriptive sense, without in any way wishing to criticise this most enterprising and commendable work on the part of the wheelmen.

Once, noticing a sign in front of a house shaded by great trees, to the effect that there was milk for sale, we wheeled into the yard and purchased some. I usually take a drink of water after a glass of milk, but I did not find it necessary on this occasion.

We soon after crossed the Albany County line, which was indicated by a sign over the path. Just before that we passed a curious little chapel which stood back among the trees at some distance from the road, on the opposite side from us. Beside the path there was a sign which read as follows: "Lishas Kill Church—Wheelmen Welcome." At least, that is how we read it as we rode past. Roadhouses, where refreshments could be obtained, were numerous. Here and there, near the path, a large painted sign warned all persons in these words: "$50 fine for driving cattle on this path." This regulation, it seems, is rigidly enforced, as it ought to be. Pedestrians may walk upon the path, but they are required to give wheelmen half of it, or the whole of it if the path is not sufficiently wide to allow the wheelman to pass without dismounting. We found the pedestrians whom we met to be very obliging, indeed. The cyclist in New York State is always treated with the greatest consideration by every one, whether walking or driving in carriages or carts.

The forenoon was replete with surprises for us with regard to the road beside which we were riding; and when near by Schenectady we came to a piece of the most novel road that we had ever seen; or perhaps we should say the most curious contrivance for getting over the road, which was nothing but a streak of deep sand, so deep that the road would have been practically impassable for teams had it not been for two lines of flag stones laid parallel to each other so that the wheels of vehicles would roll along upon them. At the first sight of this wonderful example of nineteenth century progress, as exemplified in New York State, we dismounted, unpacked the camera, and took a photograph of it. A party of ragged small boys who were playing in a disused dwelling flocked over to watch the operation, and took pains to stand where they thought they would be in the picture, each with his mouth open. We requested them to stand out of the way, as we were not photographing zoological freaks while on this tour; but one of them managed to get within the field of the camera. The Junior Partner, wishing to reward this boy for his calm perseverance, told him that if he would tell her his postoffice address, she would send him a picture. As he did not seem to know what "postoffice address" meant, the Junior Partner asked if he knew where his father's and mother's letters came; but he did not. He had never heard of Boston, and did not know that New York had been annexed to Long

Island; and all within about ten miles of the classic halls of the capitol at Albany.

As we entered Schenectady we had to take to the streets, which were in pretty good condition. At any rate we managed to worry along by keeping close to the curbstone a part of the way. At the foot of the hill we crossed the bridge over the Erie Canal, and, as it happened, a line of boats was coming along bound east; the tow horses moving slowly along at the end of a long line called the tow-line. We dismounted to watch the boats go under the bridge; evidently one of the boatmen had gone ashore to procure supplies, for, as the boats passed under the bridge he lowered down, by means of a cord, a large tin pail of milk, and then let himself drop upon the deck of the moving boat.

From the brief glance at Schenectady which we allowed ourselves at this time, we do not feel qualified to pass judgment upon the city.

Stopping only long enough to get dinner, we returned to the canal, and descending, with the wheels, a long flight of steps between the abutment of the bridge and a building, we stood upon the tow-path. It had the appearance of being a very good road for the wheels. Although called a "path," it is really a broad road-way; as wide as the average carriage road, and as we mounted and started westward it promised to be very good, with a fairly smooth surface.

The first sight of the canal was very interesting to us. It is a wonderful work, and even in the present time of improved methods and facilities, it would be a most wonderful piece of engineering. The great artificial water-way reaches from Buffalo, at the western end of the state, to Albany, at the eastern end. It's length is three hundred and fifty and one-half miles, and its total cost was $46,018.234. Projected and constructed before the days of steam railroading, it furnished direct water communication between the great lakes and the Atlantic seaboard, through the medium of the Hudson river, which it joins at Albany. It was the first great connecting link between the east and the west; and at the time of its completion it furnished what was then thought to be very rapid communication between the great lakes and the Atlantic ocean. And the era of steam railroads has not rendered the Erie Canal obsolete. In these days it teems with activity, and each spring, summer and autumn, throughout its entire length, the boats dot its course, constantly passing east and west, loaded with grain, lumber and other products of the west, and taking back to the western terminus the products of the eastern country.

The canal is very pleasing in its general aspect, the banks being neatly walled up, and the waterway itself is "brim-full" of water.

We very soon saw boats coming from the opposite direction, and when within a few rods of the tow horses we dismounted so as not to frighten them, and stood beside the path until the horses had passed. The horses draw the boats by a line, about a hundred feet long, made fast at the bows. Usually there are two or three boats in line, made fast to one another by lines, the tow-line being made fast to the first boat. Three horses usually constitute a "tow." A man follows behind the slowly moving horses. I said to one of the tow-boy-men—"you're on a pretty long walk, aren't you?" The man, cheerful from his dusty boots to the slouch hat which shaded his sunburnt face, replied that he was nearly to the end of it then.

The tow-horses are changed at intervals, sometimes being taken on board one of the boats while fresh ones take the tow-line, while at other times the changes are made at stables by the canal. The crews live on board the boats, many of them with their families. They live, cook, eat and raise families as they float back and forth through the canal. Children are born and reared on the boats. It is an interesting sight to see one of the boats floating past with the members of the family, occupied with their daily duties just like people who inhabit stationery domiciles. Children are running about the deck; the mother, and perhaps some of the daughters, are getting the meals ready, to the merry rattle of dishes and the odor of cooking, or else the family washing is being done, the clothes being hung to dry on lines strung over the deck. Each boat has a deck-house which serves as a dining and general family living-room. The kitchen is below the deck, as are also the sleeping bunks; but during the warm weather the boat people sleep under awnings on deck, or in the living room of the deck-house.

The canal-boat men are, as a whole, a curious conglomeration. All are rough in appearance and some are positively villainous looking, and are fully as hard characters as they appear to be. Others, though naturally rough on the exterior, are really kind-hearted and not bad men at all. Some of them appear to enjoy meeting tourists along the way while others will scowl at strangers whom they meet on the tow path.

The boats are long and narrow and very blunt, both ends being exactly alike. Naturally they draw comparatively little water. Through the open hatches of some of them we could see the nature of the cargoes. One we noticed carried lumber, and another had grain in bags. The boats really go faster than they appear to, at the first glance, for it requires only about ten days to cover the distance of 350 miles, an average of 35 miles per day.

In its course across the State, the canal, of course, has many different levels, being much higher in the center of the state than toward either end. The boats pass from one level to another, up or down, by means of locks, and the passage of the boats through the locks, and the manipulation of the locks are very interesting.

The canal, being at different levels, cannot be supplied with water from either terminal. This is accomplished by what are known as "feeders;" natural streams that are tapped so that a portion of their waters flow into the canal, taking the place of that which flows out through the operation of the locks, thus keeping it constantly filled with water.

The course of the canal is through the beautiful Mohawk Valley, following very nearly the course of the Mohawk River along the right bank, between the river and the line of the West Shore railroad. The Mohawk Turnpike—that great thoroughfare across the Empire State—follows the course of the river on the north side, while, between the turnpike and the river, is the New York Central railroad.

The Mohawk Valley, which we had just entered,

is a broad rich intervale, a most beautiful and fertile country, with level meadows and cultivated farms, lofty hills and mountains rising on either side.

Through this, one of the richest and most superb sections in the entire country, the Mohawk river winds like a ribbon of silver, reflecting the beauties of the verdant valley, making a picture which is beyond the power of either pen or camera to describe.

CHAPTER III.

Canal Locks and How Operated.—An Anxious Moment Followed by a Repair to a Tire.—The Tow-Path Abandoned. On the Mohawk Turnpike.—Through Amsterdam to Tribe's Hill.

A FEW miles along the canal and we saw the first lock. At first sight it looks something like a dam. The path rose by a sharp grade from the lower level, on which we were wheeling, to the upper, the drop here, or the distance from our level to the other being eleven feet. The lock is divided into two parts by a solid wall of masonry built longitudinally in the centre of the canal. At either end of both the sections thus formed are massive gates of heavy beams and planks. The combined structure forms the lock—or, rather, two locks, one being used to pass the boats from the lower to the upper level, and the other from the upper to the lower.

On the great wall which separates the two locks were small buildings used as offices and store-rooms. On the opposite side of the canal, among great spreading trees, stood the home of the keeper, his family and assistant. One can walk across the canal, from one side to the other, over the gate-heads and the central wall.

We stood looking at the locks, when the keeper

invited us to step across to the centre and sit in the shade of the buildings and trees, where chairs were placed. Leaving our wheels in some tall weeds by the side of the tow-path to protect the tires from the sun, we accepted the invitation and crossed over.

In a few minutes we were pleased to see a tow of two boats coming along the canal, for we were anxious to see them pass through the locks. The keeper and his assistant were very courteous to us, and explained the process as the boats went through. They were going from the upper to the lower level, and they went astonishingly quick. The lower gate was, of course, closed, so the water in the lock was at the same level as that in the upper level of the canal. Just as the tow-horses reached the lock the tow-line was slackened and carried over the timber work to the lower level, where the horses stopped. Slowly the two boats glided into the lock, and were stopped. Then the keeper, going over to the lower gate, turned a wheel, whereupon the water began to rush and foam under the gate as it escaped to the lower level of the canal. At the same moment the boats began to settle rapidly. The lock gates are not opened until the water in the lock has settled even with the lower level; but it is allowed to escape gradually through a small sluice-way at the bottom. When the water ceased to bubble out of the lock the keeper stepped back to the other end, and, with a turn of another wheel started a small turbine water-wheel which furnished power for swinging open the great lower gates. Then the tow-horses were started, the line again became taut, and the boats moved on once more, eastward. After they had passed out the lower gates were again closed, and the water was let in from the upper level until the lock was filled, ready for the next tow of boats. In "locking" boats from the lower to the upper level, the process is simply reversed.

We enjoyed a pleasant chat with the keeper and his assistant, sitting in the shade of the buildings where we could look both up and down the superb water-way, and across the beautiful valley; then, after taking a photograph of the keeper, his wife and little girl and assistant, we bade them good-bye and returned to the tow-path and prepared to re-mount the wheels.

Happening to glance at the rear wheel of my machine, something caught my eye which caused cold chills to creep over me. The tire, for about two inches close to the rim, was split, and the inner part was bulging outward with the pressure of the air inside. Many cold and clammy thoughts chased one another through my mind in rapid succession. I pictured our position, miles from a repair shop, with an unridable tire, and all at the very beginning of our journey. I saw the cause of it all. The tire had become worn, but it did not show until it had been subjected to the unusual strain of going over bad roads. Then it had given way. Being experienced cyclists, we had with us two full repair outfits, one with each wheel, and, following the suggestions of the Junior Partner, I at once began to repair the tire. I first took one of the pure rubber-gum patches, pulling and working it out into the form of a thin ribbon, long enough to cover the split. I then carefully wound it with tire-tape, and over the whole, having first deflated the tire a little,

I laced a rubber tire-band. The tire was then pumped up and we resumed our journey. Here I wish to state that this accident to the tire was a very serious one, not only from the nature of it, but on account of our situation at that time; yet I rode it about 300 miles, simply putting on two new patches and new tape as it worked off the break, and once supplying a new band when the first one put on had worn through.

As we rode along, the tow-path became rough and the wheeling was hard. It had the appearance of being a good road as we looked at it from a distance, but it was covered with small stones, ranging in size from small pebbles to stones as large as eggs. In some places the path had been recently repaired, which made the wheeling even worse. Once or twice we came to gangs of workmen engaged in making repairs, and we could not help being impressed with the care which is taken of the canal property.

We made slow progress, and a short distance further on we came to another lock, just after passing which another tow of boats came slowly around a bend. Both banks of the canal are very attractive on account of the profusion of beautiful trees and shrubs. Frequently we would pass under a bridge which carried the highways over the canal. The third line of boats which we met was not preceded by horses, and at first we did not exactly know what to make of it. But, as it came nearer we saw that the head boat was propelled by steam, having a regular propellor, and that it was towing the other boats.

We were beginning to weary of the tow path,

although it was so interesting along the canal, for it was very rough on account of the small stones. We were also getting very thirsty. Seeing a farmhouse just ahead, we left our wheels near the abutment of a bridge which spanned the canal, and going around to the other side of the fence, into the farm-yard, we asked permission to get some water at the well-house, which we noticed under the large shade trees. The water was deliciously cool, and we felt greatly refreshed. We then inquired of the woman at a window of the house if we would be able to cross the Mohawk river thereabout, and reach the turnpike; for we decided, if possible, to leave the canal for a time as we were making very slow progress. She directed us down the road just ahead, which led to the right, telling us that we would soon come to the end of the railroad bridge over the river, which she pointed out to us a short distance across the meadows. She informed us that people were accustomed to cross on the railroad bridge, on foot, as there was no highway bridge near there. We thanked her, and going back to our wheels, seeing another tow of canal boats approaching, we stepped into the shade under the bridge and unpacking the camera, took a photograph of the canal with the approaching tow.

On the stone abutment of the bridge we noticed this mandate in red characters: "Prepare to Meet Thy God; Watch & Pray." We did not stop to investigate the reason for this warning, but going up on the highway we wheeled northward over a very good stretch of road, and in a few minutes came to a small place, important, apparently, chiefly because it was an important rail-

way junction or terminus; for there were many tracks, and railroad buildings, many trains and much switching of cars. It soon dawned upon us that this place was Rotterdam Junction, the western terminus of the Fitchburg railroad.

We inquired of one of the railroad men about going over the bridge, and he told us that it would be perfectly safe as soon as a train then ready, went out, going east. So we followed the train, walking beside the track leading our wheels; but just as we reached the end of the bridge we saw a train coming over it toward us. We waited for it to pass and started over the bridge, walking on the ties which were very close together.

The water in the Mohawk here was very low and the bed of the river seemed to be nearly dry; but the stream was wide and shallow and doubtless there was more water in it than we realized. The Junior Partner walked very gingerly for the bridge was high above the river, and the water far below was unpleasantly visible between the open-work over which we walked.

A short distance from the other end of the bridge we turned to the left and followed a road across a field, to a barn which we saw in the direction of the turnpike, where some men we e unloading hay and stacking it outside in the yard. We were told to go through the barn to the yard in front, which we did, stopping at the well to get a drink of water; and then we stepped out to the turnpike.

Like all turnpikes that we had seen while touring this one was poor. It was so rough and sandy that we should have been worse off than if we had remained on the tow path, had it not been for the excellent cinder path made by the wheelmen. But on the path the wheeling was superb, and we flew along at an exhilarating speed. The scenery along the way was very attractive, with pleasant-looking residences, cultivated estates and fine trees. This particular region did not appear to us to abound in cultivated fruits, except apples, of which we saw some fine orchards. We met numbers of local wheelmen and usually gave them the benefit of the doubt—as to their skill in riding.

The progress which we were now making was quite satisfactory, and we reached Amsterdam at three o'clock. We did not dismount, but rode through the town by way of the main street, which was broad and quite smooth.

Amsterdam appeared to be a wealthy, prosperous town. It is built on a level plain, between the hills on the right and the Mohawk river on the left. As we passed the outskirts we noticed some fine residences with extensive grounds, parks and lawns. The cinder path continued for most of the way, with now and then a short break, when we followed the road. But such places on the turnpike were usually quite good, and we rarely dismounted. The only unpleasant feature of the ride was that we had to ride one behind the other nearly all the time while following the narrow path, which, a good deal of the way varied from a few inches to a foot or two in width.

We passed several signs by the path, put up by the League of American Wheelmen. One of these bore this inscription: —"Join the League and wear the badge; your money will help to make this path better," and we blessed the League all the way as we glanced at the wretched road which masquerades as the great main thoroughfare across the State of New York.

Stopping at a small place called Tribe's Hill which was reached after a sharp climb on foot, we rested a few minutes at an inn, and refreshed ourselves with glasses of milk. We had determined to go to the next large town, Fonda, and there to stop for the night. The inn-keeper at Tribe's Hill gave the distance to Fonda as eighteen miles, but we afterwards found that he must have willfully prevaricated, thinking thereby to secure us as guests at his own house, which, by the way, did not bristle with attractiveness, so far as we could observe.

As we started to descend Tribe's Hill, we noticed a sign, placed there by the League of American Wheelmen, which read: "Dangerous to Ride Without a brake;" and another:—$50 fine for driving on the cycle path."

CHAPTER IV.

Fonda to Spraker's.—Stop at Palatine Bridge, Where a Tire is Repaired.—We Dismount at Fort Plain for Dinner.—Interesting Scenery on the Way to Little Falls.

WHEELING easily along toward Fonda, we enjoyed rare views of the scenery, the beauty of which was enhanced by the illumination from the declining sun, which caused the trees to cast long shadows across the valley and the river. We were going along parallel with the four-tracked line of the New York Central railroad, along which trains dashed by, going either east or west; and we saw several novel engines drawing what we presumed were local trains. These curious engines were more like motors than locomotives, having the appearance of street motors used for shifting cars in large cities. Looking to the left, beyond the Mohawk, we could frequently see tows of boats moving along the canal; and beyond, now and then, a train spinning along the West Shore railroad.

We met other wheelmen frequently, and, in each case, the rarest fraternal courtesy was extended to us. Passing constantly through so many interesting scenes, we regretted that we were obliged to ride in "Indian file," for we could not readily converse. Occasionally we would dismount in order that we might more fully enjoy some particularly entrancing view.

The river, now reflecting the dark shadows and the brilliant coloring of the setting sun, was constantly in view. The day had not been hot, but, on the other hand, very comfortable; nevertheless, we felt dusty and in need of an abundance of water and towels when we rode into Fonda, at just eight o'clock, where we were directed to a hotel. It was typical of the "hotels" encountered all through this region, its principal income being derived from the bar-room. But we were shown to a large, neat and well furnished room, and after removing the dust, we announced ourselves as being ready for supper. While the supper would not have been received with wild joy by less hungry people than ourselves, we did it ample justice, and really it was not bad, considering the lateness of the hour. But it occasioned not a little spluttering in the kitchen. All hands did their best to serve us, however, and we did not complain very bitterly. After supper we unpacked the wheels, and then went out for a walk along the main street. It was a quaint sort of place, with the streets dimly lighted, and some of the stores looked musty, like curiosity shops. Fonda is a town of about twelve hundred inhabitants, and its industries consist of a knitting mill and a broom shop. It also has some good-looking girls. The railroad station was situated directly in front of our hotel, and we anticipated plenty of noise during the night. In this we were not disappointed, for there was a continued rattle of trains and blowing of whistles.

A line of electric cars had its terminus near the

railroad station. On the cars were the initials of the road: "F. J. & G. R. R." I tried to make out the name, which I finally decided must be "Fonda, Jerusalem and Gethsemane Railroad;" but it turned out to be "Fonda, Johnsonville and Gloversdale"—electric branch.

Before we retired for the night we sat for a time on the verandah of the hotel, after which the Junior Partner changed the plates in the camera, taking fresh ones from the touring case and packing away those that had been exposed.

The morning dawned bright and pleasant, and after breakfast we fastened the luggage to our wheels and started for Herkimer, stopping at the post office as we left the town, to mail letters and papers. We were in good spirits, and for the first four miles we found very good wheeling on the turnpike. The river looked more beautiful than ever, winding through the green valley. Lofty hills rose from the very edge of the road, on our right, covered with thick, rich vegetation. We saw quantities of delicious thimble berries, and often dismounted to gather them. Shortly after ten o'clock we reached Yost's, a small railroad station. Here, by the fence, we chanced to see growing a large quantity of catnip, and the Junior Partner, remembering our large, handsome cat, gifted with more than ordinary human intelligence, gathered a bunch of it, which she strapped to her wheel, intending to mail it to "Gussie" at the first post office we reached. We left the wheels by the steps that led down to the station platform, and went down to inquire what time the Empire State Express was due on its flight from New York City to Buffalo, as we wished to

see it pass. A switchman informed us that we would have about time to reach Palatine Bridge, a few miles further on, where we could stop and see the express go by. The road was very good, and we rode along easily. We passed Spraker's, another small station, but we did not stop, and reached Palatine Bridge fully twenty minutes ahead of the express. This is a large and handsome town, with broad, well-shaded streets. In front of a large, beautiful estate we noticed an artistic structure erected above a spring. Some children near by told us that it was a mineral spring, and that the proprietor of the estate allowed it to be free to the public. I drank a glass of the water, but the Junior Partner would not be persuaded to taste it. The water was very strongly impregnated with sulphur, and the odor thereof was like unto dramatic eggs.

We then wheeled on a short distance, and stopped at a shop and inquired for milk. The proprietor did not sell it, but directed us to a house a short distance further up the street, where we were given a hospitable welcome, invited into the house by a thrifty looking young matron, who brought us all the rich, creamy milk we could drink, and absolutely refused to accept payment. While we always hold ourselves in readiness to pay for everything we get, and a good deal that we do not get, we have never met with such hospitality along the road in Massachusetts. It is common for the country people of Nova Scotia to refuse payment for milk which they will always offer you when you ask for water, and it is of very frequent occurrence in New York State and in Vermont. But not so with your Massachusetts Yankees, "not by a gosh darned sight.

Ef them city folks haint gut nothin' t' dew but ride 'raound on by-cic-les, let 'em pay fer what they git; haw !"

Thanking the lady for her kindness, we hurried back to the end of the bridge which crosses the Mohawk here, and then turned sharply to the left, down the hill to the station. We learned from the baggage master when the Empire State Express was due, which would be in a very few minutes, and finding out which track she would come on, I got the camera ready and focused it at a hundred feet. Soon the express came thundering down the valley, taking water as she rushed along, and when she passed the station she was going about sixty miles an hour. I pressed the bulb, and then caught up the camera and sprang back so as to escape her wind as she rushed past.

That morning, just as we were leaving Fonda, we noticed that the Junior Partner's rear tire was flat. We pumped it up, but the air escaped slowly, so that it was necessary to unpack the foot-pump again before we reached Palatine Bridge. As there was a fountain of water near the station, I put the tire into it and in a moment discovered the leak by the air bubbles. It was only a pin-hole, and an injection of cement soon set it right.

Here, also, we went into the post-office, which was installed in a store, to send the catnip home by mail. The postmaster obligingly wrapped it up, and it was duly addressed with "Gussie's" name and street number, and we were afterward glad to know that he received it in good time, and that he was perfectly delighted with it.

We continued westward, finding fairly good

(36)

wheeling, with the aid of side paths, and the country through which we passed was no less beautiful. The vines of the wild grape hung in dense tangles from almost every tree and thicket, and thimbleberries were abundant, much to our satisfaction. A few miles on and we could see, beyond the river, the little town of Canajoharie, and a few miles more of side paths took us to Fort Plain, small and unimportant on this side of the river. The larger portion of the town is situated on the opposite bank, the two parts being connected by a covered bridge. The Junior Partner inquired of a woman in the street, whom she first frightened half out of her wits by ringing her bell—for the woman was occupying the whole of the cycle path—where we could get dinner. She pointed out a little inn just ahead, which we found was kept by some good German people, who made us at once feel perfectly at home while dinner was being prepared for us. It was a little past the dinner hour. The hostess made profuse apologies for not being able to give us a better dinner, but she gave us a delicious meal, the best, with perhaps one exception, that we had during the entire tour. In some way she discovered my weakness for pi , and I had plenty of it, and good pie, too, for the first time since we left Somerville, Massachusetts, for which dinner we were charged the modest sum of twenty-five cents each.

Going on, after I had enjoyed a good smoke, we found the roads very bad, rough and sandy, and the side-paths still continued a god-send. Still we were obliged to keep to the road a good deal, and being very rough, the vibration of the heavily loaded wheels was very tiring.

St. Johnsville was the next town reached. It is a large place, and we stopped only a few minutes while the Junior Partner made some purchases at a store, and I went to the postoffice to forward a letter. The road continued very poor, with some fair stretches; but the occasional side-paths continued, so we made very fair progress. Making a sharp turn to the left, the road took us close to the Mohawk at a point where the river was spanned by a suspension bridge, and a few rods further on so beautiful was the picture as we turned and looked back toward the bridge that we unpacked the camera and took a photograph of the view. Then we mounted again and wheeled on toward Little Falls, which would be the last town before we reached Herkimer.

CHAPTER V.

East Canada Creek.—Chauncy Jerome's Tavern.—A Historical Locality.—Two Cycle Tourists from Ohio.—More Wonderful Scenery.—Arrival at Herkimer.

THE road continued very poor to fair, and we had frequently to dismount and walk through sand and over rough places, while now and then we encountered stretches of side-paths, over which we made good progress. The country did not vary materially in its general aspect. All the way we were near the river, and beyond, on the canal, we frequently saw tows of canal boats moving slowly along, most of them going east. We could not see the water in the canal, which gave the moving boats a very curious effect, for they appeared to be moving along across country, winding over the meadows and among the trees.

Feeling anxious to reach Herkimer that night, and realizing that we must encounter poor roads all the way, we wheeled as steadily as possible, only dismounting when compelled to do so. The vibration of the wheels as they passed over the rough roads was a source of considerable discomfort to us, and very wearying.

Going down a steep hill, a dense woodland on the right, at the foot we came to a fork in the road. Our course lay directly ahead, the other road, to the right, being only a small one—simply a lane. We presently found ourselves on a covered bridge, the most dilapitated and antiquated affair we had ever seen. The planks were all loose, and rattled noisily, awaking the echoes through the venerable structure as the wheels passed over. We could see through the crumbling sides and up through the roof. It spanned a small, picturesque stream called East Canada Creek, and the view, both up and down stream, was entrancing. At the further end of the bridge stood an old disused toll gate. This road is of great historic interest, and, in the early days, it figured very prominently in the process of development of the country, and in the extension, westward, of civilization; for it was the great thoroughfare between New England and the unexplored West. The emigrant trains with the pioneers and their effects followed this great turnpike across the State of New York, on their way to settle in Ohio and further west. The time was, when this road was covered, so to speak, with continuous processions of emigrant trains, moving toward the great El Dorado—toward the setting sun. This was long before the Erie Canal was cut through along the other side of the Mohawk. At that time there was a ford where the bridge now spans the creek. In those early days Chauncy Jerome's Tavern, still standing just off the road near the toll-gate, flourished. In those "palmy days" of the olden time, Cnauncy Jerome dispensed hospitality to wayfarers in the good old way, and many was the high carnival held in the old Tavern. As we stopped just beyond the toll-gate an old man, dressed in a seedy, rusty, well-worn suit of blue,

carrying under his arm several musty looking books
and a camp-stool, came across the meadow from the
edge of the woods and greeted us. As we soon
found out, he was an antiquarian of considerable re-
pute, and how his old frame straightened, and how
his enthusiastic old face lighted up as he discoursed
on the historical lore of this interesting locality, and
told us all the things here related. This portion of
New York, he said, suffered even more than did
New England during the period of the Revolutionary war. He showed us the inside of the Tavern,
which is today practically as it was in the olden
time. The smoke-stained walls and the quaint bar
are there. Above the bar there was a painting of a
hunting scene in the days of the flint-lock, the pow-
der-horn and the bullet-pouch, also a fishing scene;
and we stood spellbound amid these associations of
the dawning of the present century. Speaking of
the many estimable traits of Chauncy Jerome, the
antiquarian informed us that beside being a model
landlord, he was reputed to be an excellent judge of
whiskey.

On the opposite side of the creek, in the old days,
from its mouth ran the old Indian trail to Canada.
But the sun was fast declining, and we reluctantly
bade the old man good-bye, and left him with his
bundle of books standing beneath a spreading wil-
low. We were compelled to do some fine riding as
we crossed a long stretch of road through the woods,
for it was both muddy and rough. Then ascending
a hill on foot we met two women on bicycles, evidently tourists, judging from the impedimenta on
their wheels. At the top we dismounted by a stream
which flowed from the hillside, and while partaking

of the refreshing draught two young men with bicycles also stopped at the spring. We entered into conversation with them, and learned that they were riding from Cleveland, Ohio, to New York City. They had come by way of Niagara Falls. Before entering the State of New York, they told us that they had averaged about a hundred miles per day; but they freely confessed that they had not made that mileage since they began wheeling over the roads of the Empire State. When we mentioned that we were from Boston they seemed to regard us with considerable curiosity, even amusement. Why, we could not imagine, unless it was because we both wore eye-glasses, proverbial abroad in connection with Bostonians.

For a short distance the road was a little easier. At the foot of the hill, a part of which we coasted, we passed under a bridge which carried the tracks of the New York Central over the turnpike; and then, the road swinging nearer the river, we came to a modern iron suspension bridge, spanning the Mohawk. We dismounted a few rods beyond, our route not taking us over the river, to enjoy the superb view, which we transferred to a photographic plate.

Now, on the right, great beetling cliffs of bare rock towered several hundred feet above us, and along the edge, far up in the air, like a trail over the Andes, the railroad wound around the face of the cliff, and then disappeared between the crags. Scarcely had we turned away from this grandeur when we beheld more natural wonders on the opposite bank of the river. Great cliffs of rock rose from the waters' edge, in most wonderful formations.

There were mediaeval castles, and columns and dark caves extended far beneath the overhanging rock. It was the most wonderful and the grandest bit of scenery which we had encountered in the valley.

Turning to the right we passed under another railroad bridge. Extensive excavations were being made in the road, which we were obliged to cross by means of a plank. A sharp, short climb took us to a ridable road, and in a few minutes we entered the town of Little Falls, a place of considerable importance, apparently.

We stopped at a store to purchase some milk, and while we were drinking it we inquired concerning the condition of the road to Herkimer. At first we had but one informant; but he was presently augmented by another, and another, until we were so overwhelmed with information that we feared that we should be compelled to remain in Little Falls over night. One man was so persistent in repeating over and over what he knew about the road that he followed us to the middle of the street as we mounted the wheels, and we rode away thanking him for his advice, but leaving him still talking.

We were now on the last stretch. The road was mostly poor, hilly and rough with a few fair places, until we were within about two miles of Herkimer when we encountered a good side-path, which here and there took us far up above the road. Soon the spires and the houses appeared among the trees on the plain below, and we did some smart back pedaling as we rode down toward the town. Crossing a rickety bridge, the planks of which slapped up and down as we passed over them, we rode into town; and, first stopping at the railroad station to make some necessary inquiries, we wheeled to our hotel.

We were both very tired but felt much refreshed after partaking of supper. During the evening an old literary friend who lives in Herkimer paid us a pleasant call at the hotel and after writing a few letters and looking about the streets a little that we might have some idea of this large and thriving town, we retired; not, however, until we had fully discussed our situation and our plans for the morrow. It had been our intention to turn east at Herkimer, and wheel to Saratoga by a more northern route, but the wretched condition of the roads, judging from the great turnpike and from inquiries, compelled the conclusion that it would be impossible to go through on the wheels. Further information obtained in Herkimer, to the effect that the roads we at first proposed to follow east were for the most part very sandy, and that we should, moreover, encounter sections of corduroy road, almost impassible even for teams, decided us to go back by rail to Schenectady, and thence wheel to the north.

Corduroy roads in the Empire state! Was it any wonder that we slept soundly, undisturbed by a nightmare of the usual sort. The Emp're State, the land of poor roads, the terror of cyclists. Every valley is a "vale of tears" and every hill a "wailing place" for beasts of burden.

CHAPTER VI.

Back to Schenectady.—We Stop for Dinner.—At the Aqueduct.— More About the Roads.— Through Ballston.— At Saratoga.

THE next morning, therefore, instead of fastening the luggage to the wheels as usual, we took them to the railroad station and had them checked to Schenectady, taking the carrier, camera, and the other impedimenta into the car with us. We enjoyed the luxury of having our twenty-four pound wheels carried free, as baggage, just as though we each had only a large heavy trunk. The railroads in New York State are required by law to carry bicycles free, as baggage. We were told by the baggage master that we must remove the bells, or, if they remained on the wheels, we must sign a release accepting all responsibility for their safety. As i was less trouble to sign the document than to remove the bells, we attached our signatures to the elaborate printed "understanding" (on the part of the railroad). It was our private opinion, however, that a bell is as much a part of a bicycle as a trunk strap is a part of a trunk, also that the courts would be of a similar opinion.

The ride to Schenectady was enjoyable, and we obtained flashing glimpses of the scenery which we had already observed in detail. Leaving the train

(15)

at Schenectady we mounted the wheels and set out to inquire for the road to Saratoga. This information we easily obtained, but we experienced some difficulty in getting out of the city, which, however, was largely our fault. Leaving the city, we wheeled over a fine, shaded street to the outskirts.

Here, be it remarked, the streets of Schenectady are far superior to those of Albany. After ascending a good-sized hill we found easy riding on a splendid side-path, supposing that we were spinning along straight toward Saratoga. But, stopping at a house for water, we communicated our suspicions to a woman who came to the door, and were much surprised to learn that we were on the road to Troy. There was, therefore, nothing to do but go back two miles, which we did without losing time; only to again get entangled in the streets, from which we finally extricated ourselves, emerging upon the right road after doing some fine riding, shooting between ledges of rock, and threading narrow paths, performing feats that we would not have believed ourselves capable of, and which we could not, probably, do again.

About two miles from the city, at the top of a hill overlooking the valley of the Mohawk, which here swings around toward the northeast, we came to a neat little modern cottage. Behind it a broad field and meadow gently sloped to the river. It had a pleasant verandah, shaded by Japanese screens, and a little green lawn in front. Noticing signs stating that refreshments were served there, we dismounted with the intention of securing something substantial in the line of eatables, for we had neglected to get dinner in Schenectady, preferring

to get started on our way, and trust to luck for something to eat. And we were well pleased with our decision, for we were met by a pleasant faced young woman, who, in response to our request for something substantial, ushered us into a pleasant little parlor, while she proceeded to prepare dinner for us. There was an organ in the room, and in view of our depression on account of the bad roads that we felt sure must be ahead of us, the organ pealed forth the strains of "Home, Sweet Home." The lady, as she entered the parlor, expressed herself as pleased with the music, and wished for more, but this was not forthcoming, for the reason that all our sentiments had been expressed in the song already drawn from the instrument.

After a little our hostess announced our dinner ready, with many apologies because she could offer us nothing better, it being some time past the dinner hour, but we found it to be a most delightful meal. After we had finished we sat for a time on the verandah and enjoyed the cool breeze, and after taking photographs of the cottage and the family, including the dog, grouped on the verandah, we remounted our wheels and resumed our journey.

Our way led along a very fair road, and a part of the way we followed a good side-path which took us along the edge of a steep, natural embankment overlooking the Mohawk. The path was well shaded by large trees, and it commanded a fine panoramic view of the country to the north and west. A short distance along, and a sharp turn of the road to the left, took us to the banks of the river, where the Erie Canal crosses the Mohawk by means of a great aqueduct. This is a most wonderful piece of work, for it may be easily understood that the aqueduct, which carries the vast volume of water across the river, high above the stream, must be a very massive piece of masonry. Not only this, but the aqueduct is sufficiently wide to allow for a tow-path of the usual width. On the left hand side of the aqueduct there is a highway toll-bridge; but as we could ride on the tow-path over the aqueduct without dismounting, we did so. At the end of the aqueduct there was a lock, having the greatest drop of any we had seen. Below it the canal swings around to the east, and here it is very wide. Half a mile beyond the lock the canal passes through a deep cutting, mostly through solid ledges, lofty hills rising, on the left, several hundred feet above it; and we rode some distance along the tow-path in this direction that we might observe the great work more closely. Then, returning to the aqueduct, we took several photographs, after which we replaced the camera on the wheel, remounted and set out toward Saratoga. Now we began again to meet our old enemy, the sandy road.

At the foot of a small hill, thickly wooded with pine, there was a junction of roads. After walking to the top of the hill where we could see the road beyond, we decided to follow the one which led to the right, especially as the telegraph wires, which we had been advised to follow, ran that way; but, half a mile further on, the road being bad, sandy and rocky, besides trending more to the east than we thought our route should take us, we stopped and inquired for the Saratoga road, of some men who were loading hay in a field near by. From the information thus obtained we found that the road over the hill was really the one which we should have taken, so we wheeled back a few rods, as we were advised, and followed a cross road until we reached a farm-house standing at the corner of this road and another which led toward the one which we must follow. After being served with cool water by a little girl not more than seven years old, who was immensely pleased with some small change which I gave her, we turned and followed the road to the left. When nearly to the Saratoga road the Junior Partner discovered raspberries and currants by the side of the road; and while she was gathering them I re-wound my rear tire with tape and laced around it a new band to replace the one which had worn through. I was then ready to proceed, but the Junior Partner had discovered some gooseberries by a wall in the pasture opposite, and while she went in pursuit of them I admired a beautiful young apple orchard on the other side, and wondered at the tremendous crop of hay which was being harvested all around.

Going on a few rods we swung to the right upon the Saratoga road. We were obliged to dismount very frequently, on account of the sand; yet we made fair progress. Ominous looking clouds were rising in the west, and we inquired of a woman at a farm-house if the indications were for a shower in this section. She laconically observed that she was perfectly satisfied that it was not she who had to take the chances on bicycles, and kindly invited us in to rest. This we declined with thanks, and receiving her instructions with regard to the road, we went on as fast as the sand would allow.

Passing through a little village we encountered

still more sandy roads, and where there were holes in the road they were mended by dumping in more sand, which amounted simply to filling one hole with another, so that, instead of being a plain hole, there was a sandy hole.

While we were wheeling along, for a wonder, over a short stretch of fair road, a tiny, young wild rabbit hopped across the road, stopping at the end of each hop to look curiously at us; and only a few yards further along a partridge walked leisurely across the road, showing not the least fear.

Pausing in front of a house, while conversing with a lady sitting on a verandah, during which we remarked concerning the wretched roads, the Junior Partner waxing particularly eloquent on the subject, the lady remarked, "Waal, we gen'lly hav' putty good ro'ds 'raound here," in spite of the fact that, right before her eyes, lay the miserable road where the sand was a foot deep. By the aid of side-paths we made fairly good progress, and shortly before sunset reached the village of Ballston, noted for its arrogant municipal authorities, where a cyclist, on the flimsiest provocation, will be arrested, taken into court and heavily fined. Wheelmen must be careful not to touch even the faintest edge of a sidewalk, even though the streets are a disgrace to any community pretending to be civilized. We had been posted regarding the reputation of the place, and none of our money enriched the treasury of Ballston. Had we known positively that it would have been used in improving the roads we might have deliberately transgressed the law to get arrested, in order that we might thereby benefit the cycling fraternity.

Swinging to the right as we left Ballston, we crossed the tracks of the Delaware & Hudson Canal Co., which, strange to relate, is a railroad company, and bore away toward Saratoga. The road was so sandy that we were glad to take to the side-path as soon as we could. As I turned into the side-path, a man with a tin dinner-pail stepped upon it. I rang my bell, but he paid no attention. Whether he expected that I would dismount and carry my wheel around him, or not, I did not know. If so, he was in error, for I went by him, unavoidably giving his pail a smart blow with my knee. I did not know but that he would call the granger authorities of Ballston to his aid, but nothing happened. We made fast time from there to S ra'oga, with good side-paths nearly all the way. We engaged in brief conversation with a man and woman in a carriage which the horse was laboriously dragging through the deep sand of the road, concerning the condition of the highways. The man was very friendly and sympathized with us concerning the roads; and I informed him that I had rather be a local consul of the League of American Wheelmen in Massachusetts than be governor of New York.

The first spring-house of Saratoga came into view just at sunset, and for three miles the wheels spun over a broad, smooth path built principally for the accommodation of wheelmen. We encountered numbers of cyclists of both sexes, the ladies with bare heads, spinning along the path.

Wheeling along the main street of Saratoga we went direct to our hotel. After supper we went out for a stroll along the brilliantly lighted gay streets of the famed resort of wealth and fashion;

where people with more money than brains came to show their wealth, dresses and turnouts and incidentally their anatomies. The shops are, many of them, as magnificent as would be seen on Broadway or Fifth Avenue. The streets were filled with the carriages of the wealthy and with bicycles; and along the sidewalks the rich bumped elbows with the poor and obscure portion of humanity. It was all beautiful and gay, but one could not help being impressed with the emptiness of the gay life here. The Junior Partner in one of the stores found an enthusiastic wheelman who was familiar with the road to Lake George, and we received from him detailed information of such a nature as to put us quite at ease concerning our ride on the morrow.

After a pleasant stroll in the splendid park of Congress Spring and foolishly drinking some of the water, which both smelled and tasted like sewage, we returned to the hotel.

CHAPTER VII.

Saratoga to Mt. McGregor.— top at Wilton for Dinner.— Caught by a Shower.—At Glens Falls.—"Pot Holes" in the River.—Over the Plank Road.—By the Adirondack Lake.— "From Lake George to Heaven and Back."

THE next morning, Saturday, after riding back along the bicycle promenade and visiting some of the most famous mineral springs, including the "Geyser" and the natural gas spring, we set out toward Lake George.

The road was far from good, but there was an excellent side path. The country was attractive and pleasant, and the day bright and not uncomfortably warm. Wild flowers in profusion bloomed along the roadside and in the fields and pastures. A pleasing feature of the landscape was the range of wooded peaks which appeared ahead of us, to the north. These were the foot-hills of the Adirondack mountains. To the east, also, blue peaks rose in the hazy distance.

As we wheeled easily along we soon entered the foot-hills, and the more pretentious peaks of the Adirondacks began to come into view further to the northward. Late in the afternoon we crossed a single narrow-gauge railroad track, apparently long since abandoned, for the rails were rusty and the road-bed was over-grown with grass and weeds.

This was the Mt. McGregor railway which ran to the mountain by that name, where General Grant passed the last weeks of his long and painful illness, and where the great soldier finally passed away; and it was over this little railroad, nearly fifteen years ago, that the funeral train bearing the mortal remains of one of the world's greatest generals wound down the mountain side and passed on its sad journey southward.

Passing through a country rich in vegetation, with the hillsides illuminated by millions of yellow daisies, we arrived at the little hamlet of Wilton. It was now past noon, and riding up to a pleasant looking hotel we dismounted for dinner. It was an L. A. W. house. We found the landlord to be a very genial man, anxious to do everything possible to make our brief stay agreeable, and we sat down to a very acceptable meal. There was plenty of home-cooked food and fresh vegetables from the garden. After dinner we took it easy for nearly an hour before we once more mounted and continued our journey.

Bearing away slightly to the left, we ascended a small hill to a sort of level plateau, slightly dipping to the north. From this elevated position we had an entrancing view of the distant mountains. Indeed, we were now among the Adirondacks. Close by, at our left, Mt. McGregor loomed up, heavily wooded to the summit. We dismounted here for a few minutes to look at the cottage where Grant died, still standing, well cared for, in the grove of trees a little way down from the top of the mountain. We had, during the forenoon, considered making a trip to the cottage, but finding that it

would be a long, hard climb both up and down, we concluded to be content with merely a sight of it. Passing across a meadow, in a deep green, cool valley, we found ourselves on an elevated ridge, mostly of sand. But, as our informant at Saratoga had told us, we found good side-paths, so we had to do but very little walking. The view of the distant mountains was superb. The wind was blowing strongly, but it did not greatly interfere with our progress as it was on our "port quarter," so to speak.

Down into a valley and up a hill on the other side, we came into view of Round Lake, a pretty little sheet of water, nearly circular, as its name implies. This lake is owned by a wealthy man, who allows neither friend nor foe to fish in it. We unpacked the camera and took a picture of it, with the surrounding hills and the intervening pasture, which was thickly covered with daisies.

The road continued very sandy, but the side-path enabled us to wheel steadily. We met two cyclists who aspired to reach Schenectady that night. We admired their enthusiasm, but not their judgment, if they were aware of the condition of the roads. When not far from Glens Falls, as we knew by consulting the cyclometer, we noticed rain clouds drifting over the distant mountains, and saw showers falling only a few miles away. The sun was shining in our locality, which produced some very beautiful and striking effects over upon the mountain sides where the rain was falling.

The wind, however, was blowing in our direction, and we saw that the shower must soon overtake us.

The wind now began to blow very strongly, and wheeling across a level plateau we had to exert our best efforts to propel the machines, to say nothing of keeping on the saddles.

A few drops of rain drifted along with the wind, and we began to look about for shelter. Ahead a small red building appeared, but it proved to be a small country school house, closed, and with not even a porch to afford us shelter. So we made haste to reach a farm-house a short distance beyond, where we found shelter from the sweeping rain on a broad verandah, embowered in vines and beautified by potted plants, while our wheels were placed in the carriage house. The shower was of short duration, and we were soon on our way to Glens Falls, the spires of which were now in sight. The side-path continued, leading us beneath spreading trees, and the sun being partially obscured by the clouds, we felt the refreshing influences of the shower.

We soon reached Glens Falls, and dismounted on the bridge which spans the Hudson River, here a noisy, rocky stream, furnishing power for several mills. As we stood looking down upon the rocks in the middle of the stream above the bridge, we noticed several very beautiful pot-holes, of various sizes, which we afterward found to be very plentiful around Lake George. They range in diameter from one foot to six feet, have a perfectly smooth interior, and are as carefully made as though executed by a stone-cutter. Locally, they are known as "Indian-kettles," and mythical tradition has it that they were made by the Indians and used as kettles for cooking their food. But such is not the case. They are the handiwork of nature, and were made by the action of glaciers many centuries ago, during the glacial epoch. Then this entire region was covered with ice, hundreds of feet in thickness. The Hudson River was a frozen mass from the high ridge of hills on one side to those of the other; and the erosion of the slowly moving masses of ice is plainly visible today. Every valley was filled with ice. Then came a change. The immense ice-field broke up and glaciers were formed. They swept southward, although the waters of Lake George flow in a northerly direction.

At various places the great irresistible ice-rivers met, and at their confluence vast eddies were formed. The larger eddies were nearest the junction of the two streams, and the smaller ones, diminishing in size, were strung along the general course. The ice-current carried boulders along, and these the eddies seized and whirled around and around in the same spot, thereby grinding round holes in the crystaline limestone which forms the bed-rock. These holes, after many years, grew deeper, and some of them seen today are fifteen feet deep. Some of them are isolated, while others are only a few feet apart, and unless they have been cleaned out they are filled with the muck of dead leaves of many years accumulation. Frequently there are found in these pot-holes the round stones, worn smooth, that bored the holes centuries ago. The pot-holes differ considerably in appearance. Some are cone-shaped at the bottom, while others are flat. The sides of the interior of some are as smooth as though they had been sand-papered, while others are creased with spiral grooves. Some are double at the top and end in a single chamber. Some are only two inches in diameter, but the most of them are large enough to admit the body of a man. All point directly downward.

While we were looking at the pot-holes it began to rain again, and we sought shelter in a lumbermill close by. Here we remained fully half an hour while the shower passed over. Then mounting again, we wheeled through the town, which is a pretty, though not a particularly interesting place, and entered the Lake George road. The sun began to shine brightly, and with the air cool we wheeled briskly along. We found the country more attractive than it had been during much of the day, and the Adirondacks soon towered above us, close at hand. We encountered a most excellent side path, broad and smooth, with but few "breaks," which the wheelmen were constructing. It is the intention that this path shall, ultimately, extend from Saratoga to Lake George. We saw numerous cyclists, all going in the opposite direction, however.

At a toll-gate we wheeled upon the famous plank road, which is twelve miles long. It amounts, practically, to a corduroy road, except that it is constructed of planks instead of round poles or small logs. The planks are laid across the road, and being worn and uneven, the road, while ridable, is not pleasant on account of the vibration which it imparts to the wheel. Were it not for the plank road, not a rod of the way could be ridden, for beneath it there is only deep sand.

Soon the blue waters of Lake George, long and narrow, surrounded by mountains, placid and mirror-like, a sapphire in the emerald setting of the Adirondacks, broke upon our vision, far below us, and we began to descend the mountain, finding some difficulty in following the narrow path which skirted a high precipice protected by a board fence. The D. & H. railroad station, known as Caldwell, is situated at the extreme end of the lake, where most of the steamer lines have their wharves.

Lake George village is a favorite summer resort, and has fine hotels. In the height of the season it is full of life. The hotels are filled with guests, and there are cottages everywhere, both in the village and on both sides of the lake along its entire length. Steamers ply regularly up and down, touching at many landings on both sides.

Wheeling to the hotel we were pleasantly installed for the night, and after supper, which we were in condition to do full justice to, we went out for a walk about the town. Its chief beauty is in the trees that shade the streets. Indeed, the village is literally embowered in fine forest trees. The lofty mountains loom up behind the town, and in front are the waters of the lake.

After the Junior Partner had made a successful call at a confectionery store, we went to the foot of Prospect Mountain, a short distance away at the northern edge of the village, intending to make the ascent on the inclined railway; but we found that the cars had stopped running for the day. We could plainly see the hotel and railroad buildings on the summit, outlined against the sky, looking as though they were suspended in the air. So we returned to the hotel, determined to make the ascent in the morning.

Directly after breakfast Sunday morning we went again to the terminus of the inclined railway, where we found a car ready to proceed up the mountain.

The roadway up the mountain is cleared through the thick timber, and is just wide enough for the road to pass along. The road itself consists of iron rails, about the same weight as ordinary street rails, laid on wooden cross-ties spiked to heavy timbers. The road is narrow-gauge. The cars are very much like heavy electric street cars, the seats being placed cross-wise of the car. These are inclined at an angle, as are also the platforms in order that the passengers shall be at a level while the car is being drawn up the steep mountain side. Along the track, on either side, there is a heavy guard rail of timber, so that if the car breaks away powerful clutches, by pressing outward against the wooden guard rails, will instantly stop the car. The road does not wind or zigzag but goes straight up the mountain.

The car is drawn by a cable. Perhaps it would be well, in describing, to say that there are two cars, one attached to each end of a great steel cable which runs up and down the mountain; so that while one car ascends the other decends. A powerful steam engine of the latest design, installed in a building on the top of the mountain, furnishes the power. The steel cable passes over a great drum in the engine house. As the cable is wound over this drum one car is drawn up and the other goes down. Just half way up the mountain at a point where the two ends of the cable, and consequently the two cars must be exactly opposite each other, the road divides for a few rods in order that the cars may pass.

The station at the foot of the mountain is connected with the one at the summit by an electric signal, and by telephones, the latter instruments being placed in the cars. When the car at the foot of the mountain is ready to start the station at the summit is signalled, and on being answered with an all-right signal, the car starts to go up the mountain and at that very instant the car then at the top begins to move down.

We took our places on the front platform of the ascending car, and the guard slipped the side rails into place. The car moved easily and kept a good speed. The summit station is 2000 feet above Lake George and the road is 6180 feet in length. Only about eight or ten minutes are required to make the trip up or down. As we progressed up the mountain the road became steeper and the trees, great hardwood giants, and spruce, pine, fir and hemlock, fell below us until they looked like tiny shrubs. We turned and looked back only to see the road like a tiny thread dropping away from and below us, until it was lost in the timber around the base of the mountain. Here and there we passed over a steep trestle, at an angle of almost 45 degrees, while a marvelous expanse of grand and entrancing scenery spread out around, the scope of the horizon enlarging at every yard of ascent. At times a curious sensation would come over us as we looked up and then turned and looked back at the receding track far below. At the half-way point we passed the other car going down. One more steep, sharp trestle and the car stopped at the top of the mountain and we stepped off upon the platform. After stopping to inspect the engine and the cable mechanism, we started to walk a short distance further up to the topmost pinnacle. There we found a small hotel. The wind blew a gale across the summit and it was so chilly that we turned up our coat collars. The view around was superb. On either hand we could look away for 200 miles. At our feet, to the south, lay the beautiful, placid, cool and shady waters of Lake George, surrounded by mountains; and still further south and southwest, the broad state of New York, dotted with lakes and streams, stretched away in the hazy distance. To the west and north nothing was to be seen but the dark wooded peaks of the Adirondacks, rising one beyond another until they were lost in the sky. To the northeast, beyond the towering peaks, we knew lay the waters of Lake Champlain.

On the very topmost crag we found a tiny bluebell nodding in the crisp breeze; this we picked and carefully placed in the notebook.

The descent of the mountain was no less interesting than the ascent for it was the reverse. The world below seemed to rise to meet us, and we were soon at the foot again, having made what one member of the party chose to style, a trip "from Lake George to Heaven and back."

CHAPTER VIII.

We Leave Lake George.—A Stop For Repairs.—At Bolton.—Indecision Overcome.— Hard Walking.— An Adirondack Camp.— We Stop for the Night.—The Journey Resumed.— The Climb Up Hague Mountain.

RETURNING to the hotel we prepared to continue our journey and had quite an audience on the hotel veranda as we mounted the wheels and started away. Leaving the village we took a northeasterly direction, the road following very nearly the windings of the lakeshore.

Although we were obliged to take to the side-path in getting out of the town because of the sand, for the first two or three miles beyond the village we encountered a very fair road. After wheeling a short distance we dismounted to make a few minor adjustments on the wheels, and I embraced the opportunity to re-wind my rear tire with tape which had again nearly worn through, for we expected hard wheeling that day and thought it best to start in good order. After the first few miles the road was again very rough and sandy, and, as it took us steadily up hill, we did a good deal of walking. But the morning was delightful and we had, constantly, charming views of Lake George. We met the United States mail coming on a bicycle and dismounted to give it the whole of the apology for a road.

The road grew worse and worse and our progress was discouragingly slow; so, when we reached Bolton, a landing place for the lake steamers, we seriously considered stopping at the hotel until the next forenoon and then taking a steamer to Ticonderoga, as the last boat for the day had gone. We did not really wish to do this, but from what we saw, and from inquiries, we felt that night would overtake us while yet a long distance from Ticonderoga. We learned, moreover, that cyclists did not frequently attempt the trip over the mountains, and since our return we have read some elaborate accounts of trips from Lake George to Ticonderoga, but which were not made over the road but by boat.

However, we at last decided to have dinner here, and for that purpose went to the best hotel there, a fine house with beautiful extensive grounds. The dinner proved satisfactory only as to quality; for the courses were microscopic and the waiter, an important young woman, was entirely out of place. She should have been a lady-in-waiting to Her Majesty the Queen, or something more exalted if possible. The price paid for our dinners was as much as a dozen of them were worth and we arose from the table wishing that we had sought some other and less pretentious place.

Having decided that it would be more becoming to cyclists to push through with the wheels, we started again, leading the machines and walking. The Junior Partner was pleased with this decision especially as we had been told that if she went over the mountain with her wheel, she would be the first woman that ever accomplished the feat.

It was a steady climb. Here and there we would ride a few yards or a few rods and then sand would compel us to dismount. It was up, up, spurs of the mountains and then down into valleys, sand and stones preventing our riding down as much as they did riding up hill. The mountains are heavily wooded, and had we not been obliged to walk so constantly it would have been far more pleasant than it was. Still we enjoyed it as much as possible.

At one place, which promised a few rods of riding, we mounted, and for safety, on account of my heavily loaded wheel, I was ahead of the Junior Partner. I was riding on a very narrow path, with thick grass on either edge of it. I miscalculated the width of the path a little, and my wheel, instead of finding solid ground, slipped on the grass and dropped into a ditch, only a few inches deep, beside the path. As for me, I rose gracefully (there is no doubt of it), over the handle-bars, turned a complete somersault in the air (I could feel myself doing it), and landed on my head and shoulders in a pile of sand. In the moment while I was collecting myself and trying to decide which end of me ought to get up first, I wondered if the wheel was broken, and whether the camera had been smashed. As for myself I was not hurt in the least. When I stood up I saw the Junior Partner standing beside her wheel, gazing up toward a mountain peak, and she seemed greatly astonished to find me there, for, she said, when she last saw me I was going skyward and she expected that I would come down on the other side of the mountain.

This incident proved the wisdom of my riding, with my heavily-laden wheel, ahead of the Junior

Partner where the path was narrow and the road steep; for, in this case, had she been ahead, a smash-up would probably have resulted.

Clouds, evidently showers, gave us some concern, but they kept well to the north. We passed a house now and then, and occasionally an Adirondack summer residence. Several times we dismounted to gather raspberries, which grew in great abundance along the roadside.

While going down a steep place, where, though it was very rough we were able to ride after a fashion, we saw in the edge of the bushes beside the road an organ grinder sleeping. With him was another man and a boy, also a monkey; though it may have been another boy. We couldn't say.

For most of the time we were shut in by thick woods which covered the mountain sides rising above us. The lake was no longer visible. Emerging, temporarily, from the woods, we descended a hill, at the foot of which there stood a handsome farmhouse. Just before we reached it the road spanned a swiftly flowing mountain stream. Here the Junior Partner dismounted and called attention to a measured "chug, chug," the sound coming from the bushes on the other side of the brook, where we presently saw columns of water, several feet high, rising with every "chug." This we at once recognized as a hydraulic ram, a most ingenious but very simple arrangement for applying the principles of hydraulics in compelling water, by its own weight, to force itself through pipes, up hill or in any direction. A hydraulic ram will go on working day and night, year in and year out, provided it does not freeze up; and in a lonely spot, its "chug, chug," is

decidedly uncanny. The water in the stream was so low that we were able to cross it on the rocks. After watching the water as it spouted from the ram, for a few minutes, we resumed our long walk.

There was very little variation in the scenery, and we continued our way steadily, riding a rod or two whenever we could. Leaving the open coun ry, we again entered the woods, climbing another mountain, and walking down the other side. At the foot we came to a deserted hunters' camp. It was a typical Adirondack camp, built of logs, and we stopped to take a picture of it. Over the door was the name "Pine Camp." Soon after we entered another clearing where we found another farm-house where we obtained some rich milk, which had the effect of greatly refreshing us. We passed a herd of cows grazing by the side of the road, and a little way beyond we stopped while the Junior Partner took a photograph of a distant mountain on which the setting sun shone in great magnificence. Half a mile or so along we met a family party, mountain people, who, judging from the p raphernalia which they carried, had been fishing. We stopped on a bridge which here crossed a swift mountain stream and asked their opinion as to our ability to reach Ticonderoga that night. They looked at us in astonishment and shook their heads, telling us that we could not possibly do it. For one thing the distance was too great, and there was also a great uninhabited mountain to cross, two and a half miles up and the same distance down on the other side, not a foot of which distance we could ride the wheels. Indeed, we had discovered, by consulting the cyclometer during the afternoon, that the distance had stretched out to a somewhat alarming extent.

As we walked slowly on we seriously speculated as to whether or not we should have to construct a rude shelter and camp for the night in the mountains or go into a deserted hunters' camp.

With the drove of cows following us and traveling fully as rapidly as we were, we soon came to some farm buildings, the house standing on a rise of ground at the right-hand side of the road, and the barn on the other. A courtly old man was coming down from the house, and in answer to our inquiry as to whether we could obtain some water, he opened the door of a well-house which stood close at hand beside the road, and drew us some water, cool and sparkling, the best that we had found during our trip. He expressed his pleasure at being able to serve us, and was greatly interested in our trip. With considerable emphasis, however, he assured us that we could not possibly get over Hague Mountain that night, and gave us the name of a man who resided not far from the foot of the mountain, who would probably put us up for the night. Thanking him we started on, still walking, resolved to spend the night as near the foot of Hague Mountain as possible.

Ascending a slight rise in the road, we looked away, at the left, over a beautiful valley, the lofty mountain peaks bathed in the rays of the setting sun. In the center of the valley was a meadow, through which flowed a large stream. Presently, swinging to the left, we crossed the stream, Northwest Bay Creek, over a rickety bridge, and, much to our relief, we were able to ride quite steadily. Soon we passed a little school-house nestling in the edge of the forest at the foot of a mountain, and a short distance further on a neat-looking farm-house appeared, where we were vociferously greeted by a noisy but harmless dog. Making inquiries here, we went on about two miles, when we saw another neat little farm-house standing some distance from the road, and high above it. To us, tired and knowing that we must stop somewhere over night, it was an attractive and home-like place, nestling among the mountains; and we have reason to long remember the warm hospitality which was accorded us by those kindly people. After consulting his wife, as all good husbands are supposed to do in all matters of mutual interest, we were invited into the house, and our wheels were carefully cared for. In the pleasant sitting-room, the windows of which looked out over a broad, rich meadow, we waited while our hostess prepared supper. Notwithstanding our earnest requests that she should not go to any unnecessary trouble on our account, she pleasantly replied that she was not doing anything extra; but all the time she was busy, moving about quietly and methodically, and when she called us to supper, somewhat to our relief, we found that we were to partake of the meal in company with our host and hostess. It was a delightful repast, and the cordial hospitality which accompanied it rendered it doubly acceptable; and the delicately creamed potatoes, the delicious hot biscuits and the soft maple sugar will ever remain a delightful recollection.

After supper I accompanied our host as he attended to the night's chores, and watched him as he called the herd of sleek cows; and in response they came slowly down the path among the trees from the pasture on the side of the mountain. I even went so far as to go up the lane to look for one animal which was particularly slow in coming down to the bars. The honest, shaggy dog "Jingo" was entirely competent to find the cows and drive them home; but it appeared that he was disposed to rush them too much, which was bad for the "mooleys."

When the cows were safely in the farm yard, we watched the milking and lis ened to the sweet notes of the whippoorwills in the forest.

We passed a pleasant evening conversing beside a wood fire, and then retired. The night, in the mountains, even though it was early in July, was so cool that we found two blankets and a quilt extremely comfortable.

We arose at half-past five in the morning. The day had dawned bright and there was a pleasant crispness in the air. While at breakfast we were told that there had been a white frost near by. We were much interested when our host mentioned that he was bothered by deer which came from the woods at night and trampled down his potatoes, which made us appreciate all the more the unique features of this wild, romantic region.

During the previous afternoon we had encountered some sections of corduroy road where the logs were bare; and several times we found stumps of trees in the very middle of the road. We were informed, at the breakfast table, that when a piece of road became so bad as to be nearly impassable, it was not unusual to repair it by clearing away a new road and abandoning that which was worn out! After this we were prepared for about anything in the line of novelties in the building and repairing of roads.

It was Monday morning, and the farmer, up betimes, to get the morning chores out of the way, was busy grinding the scythes; but he gave us a few minutes while we took photographs of himself and wife, the house and the dog, and then he bade us good-bye and rode away on the mowing machine towards the meadow, where the rich grass was sparkling with dew.

Our wheels were packed and ready for the day's journey, and as we took leave of our kind hostess she gave us a paper of ginger cookies, for, she said, we might get hungry before we reached a place where we could obtain food, and we had a long, hard climb before us.

Once more we were in the saddles, but only for a few minutes. It was but a short distance to the foot of Hague Mountain, which towered before us, far above the lesser peaks, bathed in bright sunshine, which lighted up the dense foliage in many shades.

Almost with the beginning of the ascent we were shut in by deep forest. Walking, and leading our wheels, we began a steady climb. As the morning passed, we were conscious that the day was getting hot, and we were thankful that the thick foliage which arched the narrow mountain road shielded us completely from the rays of the sun. It was a region of great beauty through which we passed, and we congratulated ourselves that we had chosen this route, which was affording us experiences never to be forgotten; and the Junior Partner was serene in the thought that she was the one among women to push a wheel over the pass over great Hague Mountain.

Birds sang in the deep woods. Indian-pipe and gaudy fungi grew in the damp places. Mulberry blossoms brightened the way, and butternut and walnut trees stretched their great branches above us. Squirrels chattered among the branches, and ran, scolding, along the rude fences; and once a deer started up close to the road and bounded away up the mountain. We found one little spring of cool, sparkling water, but we observed that all the mountain water-courses were dry, indicating that the season had been one of drought in the mountains.

Up, up we climbed, the road being so steep in many places that it was a task to push the wheels, and we were glad to stop frequently to recover our breaths. Only occasionally did we obtain a glimpse of the sky directly above us, and rarely did we catch sight of a mountain peak to the right. On the left a mighty wall, covered with trees, shut out all view.

The cyclometer showed that we had climbed two miles. Half a mile more, and if we knew the distance correctly, we should stand on the top of the mountain.

Another sharp ascent, up which we struggled with the wheels, and a broad expanse of blue sky broke upon our vision. We could see the tops of the mountains all around us. We stood on a grassy, level road, and we knew that we were at the top of Hague Mountain.

CHAPTER IX.

Descending the Mountain.—A Startling Discovery.—We Reach Hague.—Comments About the Roads.—Arrival at Ticonderoga.—Lake Champlain.—The "Ethan Allen."—Pleasant Wayside Acquaintances.

WE soon saw, however, that we had another short, but sharp rise to climb, and beyond we again reached level ground, but it was unridable. To the left a broad area of grass-land, dotted here and there with bushes, stretched away to the base of the mountains; several rods from the road we noticed smoke, apparently from camp fires. We soon saw that the fires had no connection with a hunter's camp, for there were men haying and the ricks were standing near by; and, as we walked along we saw a barn around further to the left.

Soon we began to descend the mountain, managing to ride a few rods here and there; but it was apparent that we should have to walk most of the way down the mountain. As we descended, the country became more open. We had, in fact, emerged into a cultivated country, divided into well-kept farms; and the landscape was here and there illuminated by fields of ripening grain. The road continued very sandy, and we therefore continued to walk, finding it even more laborious holding back the wheels while going down hill, than we had pushing them up. Very occasionally we could ride a short distance, but we would be compelled to dismount so suddenly that the headway of the wheels, combined with the sharp decline of the road, gave us some bad shakings-up, and often our feet were hurt severely. Indeed, my shoes, new when we started from Boston, had their soles worn through to the thickness of paper; so there was very little protection from the stony road on springing suddenly from the saddle.

Reaching the foot of the mountain we came to a farm-house, where we procured some milk, and with the ginger cookies which our hostess had given us, we enjoyed a frugal luncheon which greatly refreshed us. The woman from whom we had obtained the milk, when I asked how much I should pay her, replied: "Wt a'ever you like." This, we had found to be a very common way among the country people of setting a price on refreshments.

After getting a drink of water from a spring near by, and lighting my pipe, we went on, for we were somewhat anxious to reach civilization where we could get a square meal, for the support of our breakfast had sometime since vanished. The country was not particularly interesting, but pleasant and good to look upon. After walking a mile or so we found a little more rideable road, but only in short sections. At one place, where we saw a thicket of blackberry bushes, we dismounted, with the idea of refreshing ourselves with the fruit, but the bushes were barren. Swinging sharply to the left, at this point, we went d wn a steep, sandy hill, through a piece of pine woods, and soon the blue waters of Lake George appeared through the trees; and we were not sorry to see it, for it meant that we would soon be on the last stretch to Ticonderoga.

Crossing a level stretch of road, over which we rode most of the way, we soon found ourselves on the edge of a high bluff, really the lowest s ur of great Hague Mountain, down which the road wound after almost doubling upon itself to the left. Below us was the lake and the Hague steamboat landing, also the village of Hague, which is, for some reason not instantly apparent, quite a favorite summer resort.

At the top of the bluff, near the turn in the road, there was a cool, restful place, in fact the only spot which seemed particularly attractive. It was a grassy bank, under a small tree, and it was evidently a favorite resting place in that vicinity. We leaned our wheels against the bank, and, fortunately, I sat down first—or came near it—for scarcely had I touched the bank when I sprang up again in a hurry. Investigation disclosed the fact that the grass was bristling with wooden pegs, or brads, cunningly designed for "puncturing" purposes. They ranged in length from one inch to four. The short ends were stuck in the ground, and being of hard wood they would not break, and the "shoulder" would prevent them from sinking further into the ground. The effect of sitting down heavily upon one of these may be imagined. The grass would prevent their being discovered until one had been wounded by them. We carefully removed all of the brads—scores of them all through the grass—before going on, and they now repose in our cabinet of curiosities. I showed them to a prominent physician at Larrabee's Point, Vermont, who said that one of them, penetrating the body, might easily cause death, and he pronounced it the most exquisite case of country fiendishness that ever came to his notice.

After this experience we descended to the landing, in not the best humor, and without the most pleasant impressions of Hague.

At the village postoffice we stopped to send some mail and we engaged in some rather earnest conversation with the postmaster about the state of the roads. This seemed to be particularly opportune, inasmuch as we had just walked over several rods of the road which had recently been repaired (?) by dumping sand upon it. The postmaster explained the condition of the roads by stating that the taxes were not sufficient to allow of their better condition. This might be true, but we suggested that it would be a good deal better and fully as easy if loam were carted upon the roads instead of sand, as it would furnish a much better road, particularly in dry weather. I concluded my dissertation by remarking that the people in New York State were regular fools at road making, which did not seem to please him. Perhaps he was a road commissioner of Hague.

In return he furnished us with the pleasing information that it was thirteen miles to Ticonderoga. As we rode through the village and the country beyond we concluded why it was that sand, instead of loam or gravel was used to repair the roads; there did not seem to be anything else. It was a country of sand. Hague is prettily enough situated, along the beautiful lake shore, but the roads are such that wheeling is practically impossible, and driving cannot be very pleasant; and the fact that a woman in a dog-cart was dashing to and fro along the road, making the sand spin from the carriage wheels, did not serve to convince us that it was easy work for the horse any more than for ourselves.

We wondered as we came in sight of a mountain close to the lake some two miles ahead, if the road would take us between it and the lake which, from the general direction we knew would be the shortest road to Ticonderoga, "Ti.," as the natives called it, or whether it would go around it, on the north side; but we did not wonder long, for far ahead we could see the road sweeping around, in a magnificent "swoop" north of the mountain. So we continued to struggle on, still walking except in a few rare instances, only stopping once for water.

Swinging around to the right, the line of sand took us over a level country. Here we passed a medium sized cart loaded with bags of grain or meal, and drawn by two heavy horses; nevertheless, the sand was so deep that the nearly exhausted horses were compelled to stop every few feet to breathe, while the driver, in a half-torpid state, was coiled up on the top of the load. A little further on we struck a down grade, and were able to ride quite a distance, to the foot of the hill where the road crossed a small stream. Walking up the opposite hill, we again mounted and were able to ride along fairly well for a mile or two, which was the first experience of the kind since we left Lake George on the morning before. Soon, to our great joy, we were able to see the spires of Ticonderoga, away to the right. After dismounting to gather raspberries, which we found in abundance, we pushed steadily on, up a steep hill, at the top of which we mounted the wheels and soon found ourselves wheeling along the fluted and badly "bent" streets of Ticonderoga, presently dismounting at the hotel; having covered a distance of 41 miles of which we had walked 30, taking two days in doing what should have required but a day of easy, leisurely riding.

The baggage was soon removed from the wheels and we gladly availed ourselves of the privilege of removing the dust of travel, feeling that we had done all we cared to do in one day. While the Junior Partner rested, I went out and examined the town, but my explorations were not extensive and I returned to the hotel and luxuriated until supper time which, to our great relief, was not long.

After supper we went out for a walk around the streets. We found Ticonderoga to be rather unattractive. It is, of course, an old town and very historical; but beside showing its age in its old rusty buildings and its generally antiquated appearance, it is not interesting. The town is situated between Lake George and Lake Champlain, the waters of the former joining with those of the latter, flowing north to the St. Lawrence river. But, after all, Ticonderoga possesses a certain amount of fascination because of its having figured so prominently in the early history of our country and in the Revolutionary War.

The most interesting Revolutionary relic hereabouts is the ruin of old Fort Ticonderoga, and we consulted as to whether we would ride out to the ruin that evening; but as we were very tired and as the distance was two miles, we decided to forego historical researches until a more convenient time.

At the hotel we were assigned to a nice room and we should have been very comfortable had there not been a "farewell" party going on. As it was, our room was surrounded, in the corridors, by the noisest collection of young people that we remembered ever having encountered. There must have been fully a million of them all talking and hooting at once. Giving us that room was a mistaken kindness on the part of the landlord. There were some among them who labored under the impression that they could sing, which impression they proceeded to disprove much to our discomfort. Then, for several hours, we could hear a young fellow on the verandah in front of our windows, pleading with and coaxing a girl to kiss him. Apparently she declined. At last she went away and left him. Pretty soon, however, she came back, which showed "which way the wind blew" with her. I had no patience and but little respect for the young man, for he should have taken a short cut and kissed the girl who, in my opinion, didn't need to be coaxed, or she would not have returned after she left him. Whether she gave the young man the kiss voluntarily or otherwise, we do not know, for at half past one a. m., he was still pleading with her and soon the company dispersed.

As we entered the dining room the next morning the landlord asked if the young people disturbed us, to which we replied—"no, not after they began to go home." The landlord evidently saw the point, and the subject was dropped.

After breakfast we quickly got under way. It is necessary to explain here that we had forwarded our extra baggage from Lake George to Whitehall, near the foot of Lake Champlain, on the New York side, intending to wheel to that point, down the west shore of the lake; but we had subsequently found that this route would be impracticable as the road was rough and very hilly. So, being assured that we should find good roads on the Vermont side of the lake all the way down, we determined to cross the lake and take the road down the eastern side.

We escaped from Ticonderoga after climbing a steep hill and wheeling over a rideable but rough road. Two miles from the town to the right we passed the ruins of Fort Ticonderoga, an interesting pile of masonary, retaining much of the form of the structure as it appeared in the days of the Revolution.

Soon Lake Champlain appeared before us, and we dismounted at the landing of the ferry boat which plies between the New York and the Vermont sides. The lake is very narrow at this point, but it increases in width toward the north, the upper extremity being about one hundred miles away on the Canadian border. While we were waiting for the boat we took a picture of the lake.

Soon something appeared moving slowly out from the Vermont side. It came steadily toward us. It was the ferry boat; a curious craft, a kind of a cross between a catamaran and a sand-scow. We gazed at it in wonder, but hailed it as the medium by which we could escape to civilization and good roads. It approached the shore, and bumped up

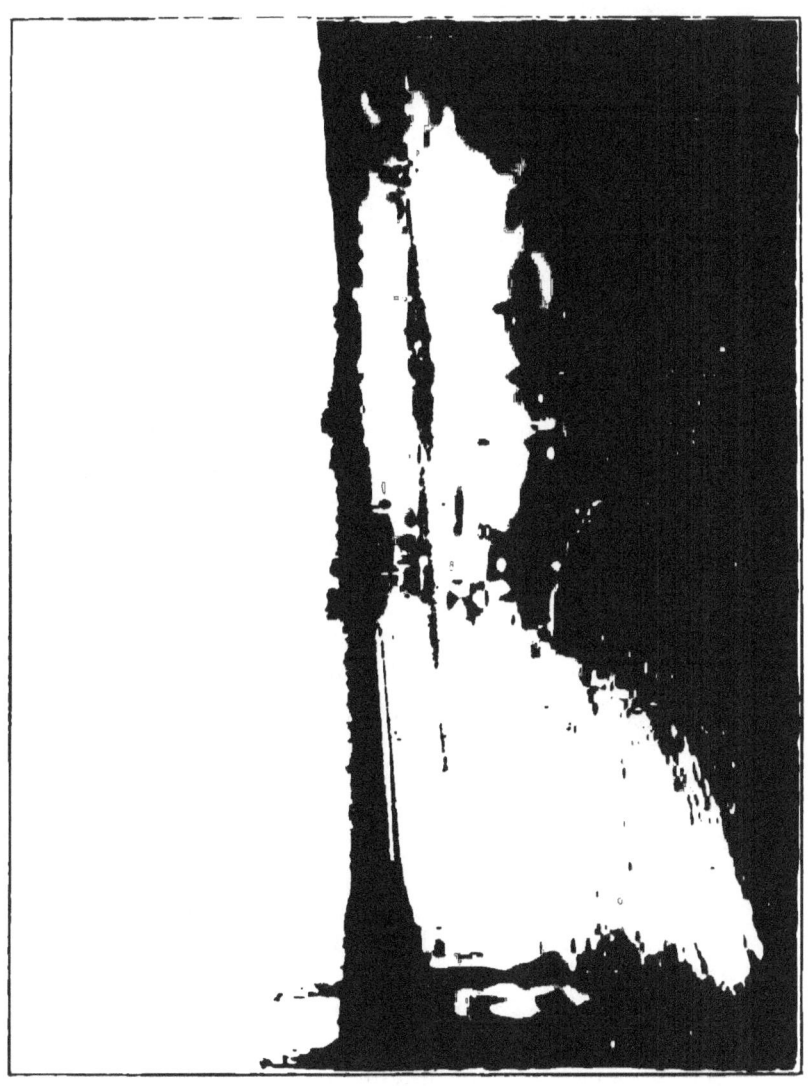

against it. Instead of being "tied up," as boats usually are, the wheel was kept revolving, thereby holding the boat up against the bank until the one horse and wagon drove off. Then we went on board with our wheels, and while the low, rakish, fore-an'-aft craft waited a few minutes for prospective passengers, we interviewed the *Multum in Parvo*. This individual was a "group," and included the captain, engineer, quartermaster, pilot, and crew. He was, in fact, a "composite," and he was the autocrat from the stoke-hole to the pilot house. I asked him if he had a state-room unoccupied, which he regarded as quite a joke. The engine and boiler was situated on one side of the boat, while the wheel was on the other. While the boat was in port the *Multum in Parvo* "fired up" for the return trip. Then he rang the signal for the engineer (himself) to start the boat, to which he responded to the captain (himself), who signalled to the pilot (himself), who, in response thereto, hustled over to the other side and laid hold of the spokes of the wheel. The "Ethan Allen," for that was her name, slowly started back toward the Vermont shore, without turning around, for her stern was exactly like her bow, and *vice versa*.

In a few minutes we bumped against the edge of Vermont, and, paying our fare, thirty cents, we disembarked, first expressing a desire to photograph the Ethan Allen. The *Multum in Parvo* obligingly suggested that I go out to the end of a pier near by, saying that he would circle around, as he went out, and come down by the end of the pier so I could get a good shot at her other and best looking side, which was the only side bearing her name. So, after he had taken a tin pail of coal on board from a pile on the shore, he "cast off," with a horse and carriage and the occupants thereof on board. The Ethan Allen circled around and came down by on the edge of a majestic curve. When she was well in the centre of the field of the camera I sprung the shutter. The man with the team stood holding the horse's bridle so as not to fail to figure in the photograph. Then we waved the craft adieu, and after watching it drift away we turned to the road. Referring to taking on coal, we were told that the captain, et cetera, takes one pailful on board at each trip, instead of taking enough for several trips at one time.

Diagonally across the road from us we stopped to make some inquiries of a lady sitting on the verandah, with the result that we met her daughter also, and the Doctor, with whom we passed a most delightful half-hour under the cool trees; for they were all interested in pursuits similar to our own, and the Doctor owned a trim little steam-launch, which lay moored in the lake opposite the house. I showed the Doctor the wooden pegs found at Hague, and we told them about our trip. We resumed our journey, feeling regret at being obliged to leave such pleasant company, with mutual wishes that we would meet again.

CHAPTER X.

Over Vermont Roads.—The Green Mountains in Sight.—Luxury of Riding.—We Stop for Dinner.—The Cuckoo and its Peculiar Habits.—Arrival at Fairhaven —A Fishing Trip.—Once More Awheel.—Wayside Experiences.—Poultney.—Granville —Salem and Cambridge.—Arrival at Eagle Bridge. The Tour Ended.—Homeward Bound.

AS we wheeled away from Larrabee's Landing we immediately began to experience the pleasure of the fine roads of Vermont. We turned south, taking the road which runs very nearly parallel with Lake Champlain, though some distance from it. It extends northward to the head of the lake, on the Canadian border, about one hundred miles away; and we were informed that the road is good all the way.

When we approached the D. & H. railroad there was a train standing on the track, the rear car being across the road. There were several of the train hands on the car, and as we approached I called out to the rear-brakeman to pull ahead so we could pass. He met my sally with the reply that he had seen us approaching so rapidly that, supposing we wished to board the train, he had stopped for us.

Until noon we spun along, not once making a dismount from necessity, past the fertile farms of this splendid agricultural state of bountiful crops and model husbandry. Meanwhile the topmost peaks of the Adirondacks, far beyond the lake, faded from view; while to the left, the giant forms of the Green Mountains of Vermont were boldly outlined against the sky.

The road was so smooth that we simply annihilated the distance, and what a luxury it was to ride easily and steadily along after our long bicycle trip afoot through the Empire State!

About noon we dismounted at a thrifty looking farm house with the intention of getting dinner. We saw a man standing by the road-side near the barn opposite the house, and to him we made known our fondest desires at that particular moment. He was a pleasant old fellow, but evidently not in authority, for he told us that if we would go up to the house with him he would see if we could be accommodated. Of course we went with him, and stood by the well-house listening to the gurgle of flowing water, while he went into the house. Presently a young woman appeared, and nothing since we left home did us so much good as the honest, friendly, hospitable smile with which that farmer's wife greeted us. She was sunshine in herself, no less bright than that which illuminated the broad, well cultivated acres around the house.

Certainly! She would do the best she could for us if we would go in; and we entered the house and waited in the spotlessly neat, cool dining room while she got dinner for us. As she went back and forth from the dining room to the kitchen she had pleasant remarks to make, and they were all accompanied by that radiant smile. It is a pity that there are not more people in this world like her; and we felt that we were experiencing the proverbial New

England hospitality which we read so much about, but which, alas, we do not always encounter.

In a very short time our dinner was ready, and such a dinner as it was! Shall we ever forget it, especially when we remember some of our experiences at the hotels in the Mohawk Valley. Nothing could have been daintier or more attractively placed before us. The linen was snowy, the silver was bright and the china was delicate. How we did enjoy it! And was there ever anything so delicious as the cake with frosting made of pure maple sugar? And all the time our hostess sat near and chatted about this and that, so the time passed most pleasantly.

Her pretty little girl was running about the room, and she came in for a liberal handful of coppers. For this delicious repast we were charged only twenty-five cents each. This is characteristic of Vermont people. They usually accommodate the wayfarer with a good meal, and twenty-five cents is the standard price. It would be rare that one could obtain as good a meal for a dollar at any hotel—especially any New York hotel.

We rested awhile, and as the farmer and his two boys came in from the hay-field for a few minutes, we had a pleasant conversation with him. Then we mounted and wheeled on. The road continued fine, and we were in the best possible spirits after our dinner. The ride was interesting, for it took us through a rich agricultural section, and bountiful crops were seen all along. Particularly was this true of the hay crop, and we were told that hay was then selling for about three dollars per ton.

Although the country was very rolling we seemed

to follow a ridge, for we were able to overlook a wide range of territory nearly all the time.

Toward the middle of the afternoon we dismounted to gather raspberrries, which we found growing in great profusion by the side of the road. The bushes were fairly bending with the weight of berries. As I parted a thicket of raspberry bushes where the berries were uncommonly plentiful, a bush-sparrow fluttered out and flew to a tree near by, where she perched and began to chirp in an excited manner. I knew enough about the habits of birds to realize that she probably had a nest in the bushes, and presently I found the tiny, cup-shaped thing, lined with horsehair. In it were four little blue eggs, those of the sparrow. But I also noticed another egg, a large one, nearly white, mottled with brown spots. Meanwhile I had called the Junior Partner to come and see it, and she at once pronounced the strange egg to be that of a cuckoo. The cuckoo is well known for its vagabond habits. It does not build a nest of its own, but deposits its eggs in the nests of other birds, where they are hatched together with the genuine ones. The cuckoo, being of a larger and stronger species, grows more rapidly than do the sparrows, until finally it crowds the legitimate offspring from the nest. The Junior Partner suggested that we remove the cuckoo's egg from the nest, but I persuaded her not to do so, for I feared the sparrow would desert her nest if we meddled with it.

It was our intention to reach Whitehall that day, and we made good time until the houses of Fairhaven came into view. We wheeled into the town, which is rather prettily situated. Just as we were entering the village a big cat came out of the grass and started to run up the road. She seemed in a hurry, so I started after her, ringing my bell furiously. We never saw such a sight as that cat was, as she ran. She couldn't go fast enough to suit her, and her hind legs flew like the prongs of a hay-tedder, making the dust fly in clouds; but she did not leave the road until she reached home, when she bounded into the yard and disappeared behind the house.

As we were entering Fairhaven we changed our plans, and determined to carry out a resolution which we had made to stop a few days and rest in some quiet place, and go fishing. So, after inquiring if the locality offered fishing, and being assured that it did, we found a quiet little hotel in a retired part of the village, where we made our plans known to the landlord, who coincided with our resolution, and pronounced it to be sound judgment, characteristic of experienced travelers. We were therefore soon settled in the "Cottage" for two or three days. The house was located in a pretty spot, with a broad lawn and vegetable garden attached. We had a fine room, and the place was home-like and pleasant. So we began the agreeable occupation of going to bed at night, getting up in the morning, eating and sitting on the verandah. I occupied most of my time smoking, and the Junior Partner consumed confectionery and read.

On the evening of our arrival we announced our intention to go fishing the next day, on Lake Bomozeen, about three miles away. The Junior Partner informed the landlord that she intended to do the fishing and catch all the fish. He smiled an incredulous smile, but kindly volunteered to help us procure angle-worms the next morning. So after dinner the following day the angle-worms were procured, and with explicit directions how to find the lake, we started on our wheels, accompanied to the edge of the village by the landlord's daughter, who pointed out the right road. Reaching the lake, after a pleasant ride, we left our wheels, hired a boat, secured a pole and line from the man on the wharf, and pushed off. Now the man from whom we hired the boat, when he found that the Junior Partner was to do the fishing, smiled a north-country smile. He was not aware that she possessed a reputation for always catching the first fish, the most fish, and the largest ones. We rowed a short distance up the lake to a place which the man suggested, but I soon decided that there were no fish there; so we rowed down the lake to a cove which I had noticed as we wheeled along the road, where I believed we should find perch. We let the boat rest among the weeds and lily-pads. I baited the hook, and the Junior Partner began to fish. It was not long before she sounded an alarm to the effect that she had a bite, and in a few minutes she had a perch in the boat. For an hour she continued, securing, meanwhile, enough for a good string. Finally we pulled down the lake a short distance to try the luck near the ruin of an old wharf; but meeting with no success we rowed to the opposite shore, and, disembarking, hauled the boat out, emptied it of the water which had leaked in, after which we secured a forked twig on which we strung the fish and then returned to the weeds and lily pads. But meeting with no further success we returned to the landing place, paid for the boat (twenty-five cents for the afternoon) and mounted our wheels to return to Fairhaven. The Junior Partner had the string of fish swinging from her handle bar, and as she passed the man from whom we had obtained the boat she held up the fish. He was no longer incredulous. A short distance along the road we stopped and the Junior Partner held up the string against the side of an ice-house while I photographed her with the fish, and when we reached the "Cottage" she walked in and confronted the landlord. He immediately adjourned to a "back seat" after making a profound bow, promising to have the fish cleaned and to cook them for our breakfast.

In the morning when we took our places at the table in the dining room, the fish were set before us, delicately browned, and the other guests looked on with envy.

And so the time passed pleasantly at the "Cottage," the pleasure of our sojourn being enhanced by the arrival of the landlord's wife, also by the arrival of another guest—a young lady from the New York side, but whose stay was, unfortunately, too short. She could talk even faster than the Junior Partner, as the landlord and his wife agreed.

Now it happened that the landlord noticed that I had, on two occasions, by winning the regard of our waitress, secured two pieces of pie at dinner. Now pie is a necessity with me—not a luxury; so when the landlord attempted to remonstrate with me, I "struck" and informed him that I must and would have pie three times a day. He saw that I was in earnest and would not be trifled with and after that

I had pie three times a day, by the landlord's express orders, which came near causing a riot among the other guests.

One day passed much like the previous one, and a favorite diversion with us was to go the postoffice when the mail came in, in the evening, and watch the people who then flocked to the office. Fairhaven has some very pretty girls, by the way.

At the "Cottage" each evening the guests would gather on the verandah and await the arrival of the New York papers containing the latest war news; and it was here that we received the news of the fall of Santiago.

* * * * * * * *

During our stay at Fairhaven the wheels received a good cleaning and I had my bicycle fitted with a new rear tire.

Reluctantly one morning, we prepared to take our departure, and the wheels packed, we bade adieu to all and once more mounted. The landlord did not believe we would be able to ride a steep hill which led out of the village in sight of the house, but we did it without dismounting, waving him a final good-bye as we sailed past beyond Castleton Creek, which drove the slate mills; for Fairhaven is famous for its slate industry, being in the midst of the quarries of Vermont; and during the forenoon we saw many slate quarries on the hill-sides, some of them being of red slate.

Again we found a beautiful road and after our days of rest we rode with enthusiasm. We were wheeling along the boundary between the States of Vermont and New York, first on one side of the line and then on the other, running great danger of

getting our pedals entangled in the "line." We were always able to tell when we had crossed to the New York side from the roughness of the roads. Wheeling through the village of Poultney, Vermont, we met a young man from our own town. He was connected with one of the slate companies and seemed glad to meet us.

At Granville, on the New York side, we stopped to inquire near the railroad station, concerning the road we should take in getting out of town. The man of whom I inquired stated that the train had gone. "But," I replied, "the road is here, isn't it?" at the same time pointing to the road and stating that we intended riding the bicycles over it. It takes a long time for the brains of some of the New York countrymen to get to work. Then he began giving us directions until a bystander, for we had a large audience, quietly remarked to another that we should have hills to climb and a rough road if we went that way, which attracted the Junior Partner's attention, who asked if there was not a way where there were no hard hills. "Oh, yes, if you want to go by West Pawlet." "That's the way we want to go," rejoined the Junior Partner, and receiving directions to that effect, we continued on our way.

Just before reaching Rupert, Vermont, we stopped at a farmhouse for dinner. We received scant hospitality at first from the woman of the house who had "ben berryin' all th' forenoon and had got badly het up;" but her daughter, a buxom girl, did her best to counteract her mother's grumpiness; so after a little while the matron began to thaw out. When dinner was ready the farmer and the hired man came in, and the former, a big son of the soil, braced up in front of me, demanding to know my name and the nature of my business. As neither was copyrighted, I furnished him with the desired information. At dinner, which was not equal to the one we had enjoyed the first day in Vermont, the farmer kept up a continuous conversation, by which I learned that the world was all askew, and that he had missed his calling. He should have been a peddler, he said. In proof thereof he related how successful he had been peddling maple syrup in the spring. He also gave us much information about maple syrup and sugar making; his farm, the crops, his son's farm, which adjoined his, and so forth. But he was agreeable and inclined to make it pleasant for us. After dinner was over, he and the hired man returned to the hay-field, and we, after taking a photograph of the daughter of the house, with her wheel, who donned a resplendent bicyle costume for the occasion, remounted our bicycles and rode on.

We stopped occasionally for water, and we were always shown great hospitality. Earlier that day we called at a house for milk, and we were served with a large pitcher full, and when we offered to pay, the woman was almost indignant at the idea of such an absurd proposition.

We rode through Rupert without stopping, for, while we had, earlier in the day, intended to wheel only to a point a few miles from Eagle Bridge, New York, on the line of the Fitchburg Railroad, we had made such good progress over the fine roads, with a strong north wind at our backs, that we believed we could reach Eagle Bridge easily that day.

The remainder of our route lay on the New York side; but, strange to relate, we found very good roads. We were now following along the line of the D. & H. road, and continued to do so throughout the afternoon.

Once we stopped at a small cottage where we saw a well, and while we drew the cool water from the depths, the lady of the house, a product of the Emerald Isle, came out to see us, wearing a pair of "sandals," which she had been carrying around with her ever since she was born. She was a good-hearted old soul.

At the large and handsome town of Salem, New York, we stopped a few minutes to try to secure at the railroad station and elsewhere, information as to the time of arrival of the Albany train, bound for Boston, at Eagle Bridge. We did not meet with great success, but we learned enough to convince us that we should have to remain at Eagle Bridge that night. So we wheeled on easily, and while 'the country was rather attractive, it was not so enticing as was Vermont.

At Cambridge, New York, a large and handsome town of broad, level streets, and fine residences, we stopped for lunch at the establishment of a solemn-faced German. Just before, however, while I wheeled ahead to make an inquiry, the Junior Partner hailed a milk-man, who gave her the information we desired. He also served her with milk in the portable rubber cup which we carried, and when she went to pay him he said that when milk was only four cents a quart he did not know, for the life of him, how he was to charge for so little.

After our lunch we wheeled on, making our best

time toward Eagle Bridge, only stopping once to gather a fresh supply of catnip to take home to "Gussie."

Just at sunset Eagle Bridge came into view, and at the foot of a steep hill we swung to the right and wheeled along the river bank, turning to the left to cross the covered bridge. On the bridge we met an impertinent bumpkin, who inquired of us, each in turn, "how fur we had rode," receiving, in reply, information which was more applicable, in his case, than that which he sought.

On the other side of the bridge we wheeled directly to the railroad station, where we learned at what time the Boston train would arrive in the morning. We also secured our extra baggage, which had been ordered forwarded from Whitehall, while we were in Fairhaven; after which we crossed the street to the hotel, none too attractive on the exterior, though we were served with an appetizing supper and given a good room. At the supper table we met a drummer for a Troy house, who gave Boston a terrible raking, saying that it was an impossibility to find one's way about the streets without a guide. He knew Boston like a book; but, much to our surprise, he allowed it to leak out that he had never been in Boston in his life! After supper we stepped into the post office, next door, and sent word to Fairhaven of our arrival, having covered fifty-three miles that day easily; then, after sitting on the verandah until we were driven in by the clouds of dust raised from the street by the passing teams, we retired.

* * * * * * *

Our tour, with its novel and pleasant experiences,

that we shall remember longer than the rough places, was ended. We had seen much which interested us and had gained much information beside going over a route not frequented by tourists in its entirety. In the morning the wheels were checked, our impedimenta made ready and soon we were seated in the train and were being borne swiftly over the good old Fitchburg Railroad, past the Berkshire Hills again, through the Hoosac Tunnel and then through the length of Massachusetts, toward Boston.

THE END.

www.ingramcontent.com/pod-product-compliance
Lightning Source LLC
Chambersburg PA
CBHW020116170426
43199CB00009B/545